D1521864

"I'd Have My Life Unbe"

Thomas Hardy by Augustus John (Reproduced by Permission of the Syndics of the Fitzwilliam Museum, Cambridge)

"I'd Have My Life Unbe"

Thomas Hardy's
Self-destructive Characters

FRANK R. GIORDANO, JR.

The University of Alabama Press

Permission to quote copyrighted material is acknowledged as follows:

Passages from "Eustacia Vye's Suicide," by Frank R. Giordano, Jr., from *Texas Studies in Literature and Language*, vol. 22, no. 4, pp. 504-19.
Passages from "Farmer Boldwood: Hardy's Portrait of a Suicide," by Frank R. Giordano, Jr., *English Literature in Transition: 1880-1920*, 21:4 (1978).

Library of Congress Cataloging in Publication Data

PR
Giordano, Frank R., 1942–   4757
 "I'd have my life unbe".   C 47
                                               G 56
 Bibliography: p.   1984
 Includes index.
 1. Hardy, Thomas, 1840-1928—Characters.
 2. Hardy, Thomas, 1840-1928—Knowledge—Psychology.
 3. Suicide in literature. I. Title.
 PR4757.C47G56   1984   823'.8.   83-1230
 ISBN 0-8173-0174-7

FOR MARGARET, GREGORY,
SUSAN, AND CHRISTOPHER

Contents

vii

CONTENTS

Abbreviations

Published sources frequently cited:

CP	*The Complete Poems of Thomas Hardy*
L	*The Life of Thomas Hardy*
LN	*The Literary Notes of Thomas Hardy*
M	*Man against Himself*
PW	*Thomas Hardy's Personal Writings*
S	*Suicide*
YH	*Young Thomas Hardy*

Titles of Hardy's novels:

FMC	*Far from the Madding Crowd*
J	*Jude the Obscure*
MC	*The Mayor of Casterbridge*
RN	*The Return of the Native*
T	*Tess of the D'Urbervilles*
W	*The Woodlanders*

Preface

W H I L E   R E A D I N G , teaching, and writing about Thomas Hardy over the past decade and a half, I have continually wondered at his emotional capaciousness and his technical versatility. He has been described by critics as a pessimist, a meliorist, a tragedian, a humorist, a realist, a romanticist, an antiromanticist, a symbolist, a love poet, a poet of despair, an agnostic, and a writer with a theological obsession. In the playful words of his own brief poem, he describes himself as "so various":

> All these specimens of man,
> So various in their pith and plan,
>   Curious to say
>   Were *one* man. Yea,
>   I was all they.

Author of several major novels, hundreds of lyric poems, scores of short stories, and an epic-drama which may be this century's greatest long poem, Hardy is unique among English authors in the magnitude of his achievements in both fiction and poetry. It is little wonder, then, that Hardy commands so much interest among the "common reader," listeners to radio productions of his works, and viewers of television and film adaptations of his stories and novels. Hardy societies in England, Japan, and the United States attest to his stature as a classic with worldwide appeal, worthy of and requiring the attention of scholars and critics wherever English literature is read and studied.

An author so widely studied and written about might be expected to be well known and generally understood, but precisely because of the range of Hardy's activities as an artist there is (every year, seemingly) a flood of scholarly essays and critical books in Britain and the United States that offers new insights about the man and his work. Though Philip Larkin's "advertisement" of 1966 ("Wanted: A Good Hardy Critic") has brought many first-rate commentators into the market, and though Ian Gregor's query "What kind of fiction did Hardy write?" has elicited substantial responses (including his own fine book), there is still much scholarly and critical work to be done with Hardy's art. And while it is unlikely that a volume of ordinary proportions will ever encompass the range and depth of Hardy's achievements, we can anticipate a continuous flow of studies (floods, mercifully, cannot last forever) dealing with themes or techniques associated with specific works or genres.

This present study of the self-destructive characters in Hardy's major fiction, limited to a discussion of the early years of his publishing career, reflects what J. O. Bailey has called "the pessimism of his first phase," as most of Hardy's novels were written before he fully developed his tentative impressions about "meliorism." Elsewhere, Bailey has written that "Hardy was probably serious in considering renunciation and even suicide as at least philosophically superior to the endurance of the world as it is, if there be no hope for its amelioration."[1]

That he was serious in allowing man the choice to commit suicide I have never doubted since the first time I read *Jude the Obscure*. But Hardy was serious about *many* things, including evolutionary meliorism, "loving-kindness," and other simpler "great things"; and his advocacy of the value of these ideas and experiences has mitigated the bleakness of his occasionally desperate vision and provided his works with the emotional and intellectual balance that has assured his continuing appeal. Nevertheless, my interest in his art has been focused on his sense of the fragility of human life, the emotional pain that man must endure in this irrational world, and man's paradoxical will to intensify his suffering— even to take his own life when his suffering becomes unbearable or his future seems hopeless.

These concerns emerged from my reading of the fictions initially, but they became subjects for my research when I realized that, over the decades, numerous scholars had spoken of the *suicides* of one or another of Hardy's characters. Some of Hardy's best modern critics, such as Albert Guerard, Irving Howe, Ian Gregor, and J. Hillis Miller (and others), have called attention to the self-destructive behavior of some figures, the masochistic strain and self-defeating passivity of others, the retreat from vital existence into a catatonic state by still others. One of Hardy's most authoritative biographers, Robert Gittings, states that after the suicide of Horace Moule, Hardy always portrayed figures who were "maimed by fate"; and he allows that a case can be made that their downfalls are caused by what I perceive as their self-destructiveness, namely, their "weakness or foolishness or rashness of choice."[2]

The burden of much of this study is to establish that position precisely. Since other critics have demonstrated how Hardy "loaded the dice" against his tragic figures, how he "victimized" them by external forces beyond their control, I have sought to understand the nature and degree of the characters' complicity in their misfortunes and deaths, for it is not external circumstances alone—not simply "Chance" or "Fate"—that account for the deeply felt tragedies in Hardy's novels. This inquiry led me to raise a number of questions. How pervasive, in fact, is self-destructiveness in Hardy's novels? Through what artistic means did he embody his conviction that renunciation and suicide are preferable to the endurance of life's irremediable evils and unabating pain? What personal and broadly cultural and intellectual factors account for self-destruction in his works? To what extent do a character's self-destructive impulses conspire with external forces in leading to his or her death? And how seriously are we to take Hardy's prophecy about a coming *universal* wish not to live?

These were among the questions that helped me define my book's chief subject, and my concentration on Hardy's most desperate, darkling theme accounts, in part, for the little I have to say about his humor or meliorism or any of the "great things" he so valued. My intention in avoiding such subjects is not to deny or minimize their importance, nor to create the illusion that I have discovered a "new" Hardy or the "quintessence" of Hardy. Rather, it is simply that in attempting to portray, as thoroughly as possible, a single preoccupation of Hardy's, it has not always seemed necessary or appropriate to discuss subjects that are not directly related to it and that, in many cases, have been well treated by others before me or ought to be left to others better qualified than I. Heredity, environmental forces, chance, and coincidence—all that Hardy means by "Crass Casualty" and "Dicing Time"—have over the past three decades received due consideration in critical assessments of Hardy's characters' fortunes. And this is appropriate, as a full and balanced account of Hardy must include thorough treatment of his "so various" interests. To the evolution of such an account, presumably through worthwhile essays and books from diverse authors, I wish to contribute my impressions of the novelist who understood, as very few writers have, the potency of man's death instinct.

This book has its roots in an essay on *Jude the Obscure* in which I discussed Jude's death as a suicide. In subsequent rereading and teaching of the novels and in discussions with friends and colleagues to whom Hardy has introduced me, I began to experience the sense of a pervasive wish *not* to live in many of his major figures. When I examined the ambiguous death of Eustacia Vye, I concluded that her drowning might be interpreted as fulfillment of a long-developing death wish. Then my fascination with the decline of Farmer Boldwood (surely one of Hardy's most remarkable male creations) led me on a long and exciting course of intensive reading in theories of suicide, and my awareness of the nature of self-destructive behavior was immensely broadened and enriched through the writings of distinguished specialists from other disciplines. While preparing to write about Boldwood, I began to think of a full-length study of suicide in Hardy's works.

Believing that the greatest novels are chiefly memorable for the characters they present—believing, as well, that the nineteenth-century novel, as a temporal art, deals with human identities and is primarily concerned with the processes of motive and cause and affect—I began to conceive of my study as a series of analyses of the self-destructive motives and behavior of Hardy's major characters. Complex literary characters are not created with a few light strokes of the pen; rather, characterization is often protracted throughout a whole book, nearly always in extended passages of prose. In each of my analyses, then, my method has been to give detailed discussions of the evolution of Hardy's

characters, using copious extracts from Hardy's texts. In this
way, the novels are allowed "to speak for themselves," as it
were, with Hardy's language and artistry always before the
reader's eyes.

To relate my analyses of the characters to the wider contexts of Hardy's life and thought and evolving contemporary
discussions and studies of suicide, my opening chapters
were prepared to sketch in these "backgrounds." Like most
critics before me, I have had to do a good deal of "borrow-
ing" from my predecessors; and Ezra Pound has advised
authors who incur such heavy debts to have the decency
either to acknowledge them outright or try to conceal them.
Fortunately, those from whom I've taken have been richly
endowed with critical insights and scholarly judgment, and
it is a pleasure to acknowledge my gratitude to those whose
work has contributed much to whatever value my book may
possess. Whatever errors or limitations exist are, of course,
of my own production.

It is impossible to write on self-destructiveness in Hardy
without acknowledging the seminal work of Albert Guerard's 1949 study *Thomas Hardy*, and I do so here, with
respect and gratitude. Guerard's classic book reinforced my
impressions about Jude Fawley while I was preparing my
graduate thesis, and in recent years it has served as a solid
base from which my subsequent explorations of Hardy's
characters have been undertaken. More importantly, however, Guerard's work stimulated my research into the sociological and psychological works of Hardy's great
European contemporaries, Emile Durkheim and Sigmund
Freud, and some of their twentieth-century descendants,
most notably Karl Menninger. The chief insights of the first
"suicidologists," developed during the major phase of
Hardy's career as a novelist and published after his fictions,
provide an authoritative, extraliterary view of precisely

those social and psychological forces that loom so threateningly in the lives of Hardy's modern characters. Moreover, the suicidologists have served the interests of literary criticism by enriching its technical vocabulary for analyzing the motives and behavior of self-destructive characters.

Guided by Durkheim's typology of suicide types, I have avoided the more conventional chronological approach to reading the novels and, instead, organized my study by considering the three types of Hardy's self-destructive figures. Thus I consider his "egoistic" suicides, Eustacia Vye and Michael Henchard; his "anomic" suicides, Farmer Boldwood and Jude Fawley; and his "altruistic" suicides, Giles Winterborne and Tess Durbeyfield. This approach has provided a coherent means of understanding not only what forces operate within particular individuals but also how the various figures relate to, and differ from, one another in terms of motives and actions or, in some cases, "strategic passivity."

When Hardy's fictions are examined in the light of the profound theories he anticipated, a novel twist is given to the usually condescending myth about the Wessex autodidact. Hardy was *required* to educate himself about self-destructiveness, because few writers before him understood the subject, in its social and psychological contexts, as well as he did. What is startlingly clear to one who reads Hardy in the light shed by Guerard, Durkheim, Freud, and Menninger is that the man possessed—in vast quantities—prophetic intuition, imaginative boldness, and artistic courage and integrity.

As my work on this study advanced, I received direct and indirect encouragement from many works, persons, and institutions. Footnotes, however copious, can only suggest

the worth of some critical and scholarly sources; but out-
standing studies by Jean Brooks, Ian Gregor, Desmond
Hawkins, Irving Howe, J. Hillis Miller, and Michael Millgate have so formed my thinking about Hardy that it is
impossible to express my thanks precisely. Professor Millgate's recent biography and his edition (with R. L. Purdy) of
Hardy's collected letters have given an enormous boost to
scholars' efforts to see Hardy clearly. The two-volume biography by Robert Gittings has put everyone in his debt; and
of particular value to me is his estimation of the influence
upon Hardy of Horace Moule's suicide. In his corre-
spondence and in our personal conversations, Dr. Gittings
has been exceedingly kind and encouraging whenever we
turned to what he calls Hardy's "morbid" strain.

My first mentor in Hardy studies, Ward Hellstrom, has
continued to be a firm supporter of many of my efforts.
Ward's friendship, and the friendship of Donald and Iris
Baker, Hal and Charlyn Orel, Frank and Marjorie Pinion,
Jim Gibson, and Desmond Hawkins, have enriched my life
(and those of my family) with much more than what their
books and conversations have taught me. We have been
beneficiaries of what is surely one of Hardy's greatest gifts to
posterity: the spirit of loving kindness in his dedicated
readers.

Everyone who writes a book about Hardy inevitably takes
advantage of the resources of the Dorset County Library
and the Dorset County Museum; and during my visits there
(in the late 1970s) the dedicated staffs of both institutions
reflected the enthusiastic professionalism and energetic
leadership of the late Kenneth Carter and Roger Peers,
Wessex worthies both. Patricia Carter, formerly librarian at
the Weymouth branch of the Dorset Institute of Education,
proved a friend indeed on more occasions than I can recall.
At the invitation of the English Thomas Hardy Society, I

gave a lecture in which I was able to work out some of the ideas that appear in this book; so to Tom Wightman and the Reverend J. M. Yates my thanks for a most enjoyable opportunity.

To the editors of *English Literature in Transition* and *Texas Studies in Literature and Language*, my thanks for their permission to reproduce, in slightly different form, essays on Farmer Boldwood and Eustacia Vye which originally appeared in their journals.

The University of Houston generously granted a faculty development leave and additional research funds, which enabled my family and me to spend eight most valuable and happy months in Wessex in 1978. More recently, the university provided funding to cover expenses for typing this book. Christine Womack and Roselyn Kennelly have earned my eternal thanks—and, undoubtedly, their eternal rewards— with their heroic efforts at taming what I euphemistically called the "rough drafts" of this manuscript.

My wife and children, in their cheerful obliviousness of Hardy and his works, have brightened the darkest days I spent preparing this book. With fondest memories of our rambles over the Wessex downs and through country churchyards, of streamside picnics and wine-and-cheese feasts, I dedicate this book to you.

Orientations

CHAPTER ONE

The Roots of Hardy's Melancholy

T R A D I T I O N A L L Y, critics write of Thomas Hardy's "pessimism" and "tragic vision" when they consider the tone and form of his major fictions and poetry. From about the time of the publication of *The Mayor of Casterbridge*, reviews regularly began to notice Hardy's Olympian ruthlessness toward his creations and to complain of his "pessimism." That he weighted the scales unfairly against his puppets, that he was too cruel, that his view of fate was too remorseless, depressing, dreary, disagreeable, terrible, he heard from critics and friendly correspondents alike.

There is, of course, a legitimate basis for describing some of Hardy's views as pessimistic—indeed, Hardy's sensitivity to being called a pessimist is surprising, as he must have considered the term high praise when he asked if any great poetry is *not* pessimistic. It seems clear, however, that Hardy distinguished the "philosophy" of the art from the personal temperament of the artist, and he insisted on the artist's liberty to describe those aspects of reality which his idiosyncrasy moves him to observe.[1] But the point of Hardy's distinction was not always evident to his reviewers, who considered a writer of darkling tales to be *in propria persona* a pessimist. Because Hardy often opposed what he considered Victorian society's vested interests in moral and political complacency, notes of irritation and defensiveness are often heard when he repudiates the charge of pessimism. To many critics, as even to some of Hardy's friends, it seems that the nettled author doth protest too much.

Still, the judgment of pessimism, in which Hardy detected implicit or explicit attack, often struck Hardy and many sympathetic readers as unfair and, in any case, not a helpful critical description. More appropriate for philosophical discourse than for literary criticism, the condemnatory "pessimism," proclaimed at the appearance of each of Hardy's most mature works, was a constant irritant to him. As a novelist, he repeatedly claimed to be expressing mere "seemings, or personal impressions." As a poet, his verses are often exquisite, deeply moving "moments of vision," whose inconsistencies and transitoriness were of no consequence. In neither his fictions nor his short poems is there any pretense about constructing a consistent philosophy or system of beliefs; his perennial claim was in fact just the reverse, for, above all, Hardy is the creator of tentative observations and "unadjusted impressions." He seems convinced that "the road to a true philosophy of life seems to lie in humbly recording diverse readings of its phenomena as they are forced upon us by chance and change."[2] Furthermore, he affirms that one's readings are to take the form of obstinate questionings in the exploration of reality, not metaphysical assertions. But for all his modesty, his repeated prefatory remarks and postpublication disclaimers, Hardy found himself cast as a philosopher *manqué*. He was adamant, it seemed to his audience, in taking a dark and desperate view of things.

Discussions of Hardy's "tragic vision" seem more satisfactory and critically appropriate in relation to such novels as

The Return of the Native, The Mayor of Casterbridge, and *Jude the Obscure,* but the other great fictions, one may well argue, are not tragic works; and the terms "tragic" and "tragic vision," when used in describing *Far from the Madding Crowd, The Woodlanders,* and *Tess of the D'Urbervilles,* are usually applied in an honorific sense, signifying the magnitude and seriousness of Hardy's undertaking, the intense human suffering he portrays.[3] Critically, the phrase "tragic vision" is only partially accurate as it does not describe the achievement of the six major works. The "vision" does not operate within certain books, even if we recognize that within them, implicitly, is the same outlook on life that Hardy dramatized more intensely in his truly tragic fictions.

Moreover, "pessimism" and "tragic vision" do not penetrate deeply enough to describe the effects of Hardy's major art. Nor can they account for the intensity of critical and popular reactions from some influential and respectable quarters. Hardy's friend, the philosopher and critic Frederick Harrison, finds something positively unnatural about his view of life: "This monotony of gloom, with all its poetry, is not human, not social, not true" (*PW,* p. 266). Harrison's opinion is debatable, though it receives some authoritative support in the assessment of Hardy by his biographer Robert Gittings, who sees the works as influenced by "an early thread of perverse morbidity in Hardy, something near abnormality."[4] Both critics suggest the limitations of the usual critical terms while they point to the kind of disturbance in Hardy's work that some find explicable only in terms of some aberration in Hardy's personality. What is at the root of his works, which makes them seem abnormally gloomy and morbid? And why have Hardy's works elicited such anger from so many readers?

Albert Guerard's assessment of the uproar aroused by the publication of *Jude the Obscure* suggests the comprehensiveness of Hardy's offensive vision. Guerard called it the fury of outraged optimism, mobilized by the moralistic and optimistic middle classes against one who questioned "the integrity of God in his Heaven and of human nature in its earthly prison, or of society as a noble experiment."[5] What else is there to question, after one examines the relations between man and God, man and nature, man and his fellow man? What is left to criticize after the institutions of religion, education, and marriage have been found wanting?

But Guerard's perceptive inference doesn't get to the heart of the critical issue. That Hardy's works seemed to offer no acceptable constructive prescriptions for social change and that he was a social outsider, without the "qualifications" of family or educational ties, were factors that contributed to the outcry against him, but in his probing and questioning of Victorian institutions and codes of morality, Hardy was by no means unique. In fact, the greatest Victorian writers were, perennially and almost traditionally, the severest critics of contemporary bourgeois life. The "alien" visions of Tennyson and Dickens, Arnold and Carlyle, Swinburne and Ruskin (to name some of the most obvious) come immediately to mind; and these authors are Hardy's most important predecessors as social critics. Also, by the time of his major phase as a novelist, the 1870s through the 1890s, other writers had been quite frank in their portrayal of unconventional sexual relations and religious apostasy, and in their attacks on social traditions and institutions that deprived man of liberty and thwarted his instincts for self-development.

Specifically, Hardy differs from earlier writers in the intensity of his scrutiny and in his persistence in telling the Victorians profoundly disturbing truths about their values and institutions that they did not want to hear. David DeLaura understood this when he wrote that Hardy was warning his contemporaries that "they had not yet imagined the human consequences of honestly living out the modernist premises." Hardy's eye is consistently on "the *painful* exigencies of modernism, its human cost, and not on its liberating effects."[6] Compelled by his artistic temperament to examine the paralysis of will and emotion in the late nineteenth century, Hardy presents the costs emphatically and repeatedly. Thus the most salient distinction between Hardy's art and the darker works of, say, Thackeray, Dickens, and George Meredith is that, in book after book, Hardy's protagonists refuse to endure paralysis and emotional deprivation; instead, they make choices and perform acts that are self-destructive, even suicidal.

At the very heart of Hardy's greatest writings is a sense of the fragility of man's attachment to life and the extreme toll in suffering often exacted of sensitive human beings. Life in the Godless, absurd universe is cruel; for many of its victims, Hardy believed, and repeatedly stated, it would have been better had they never been born. And while Hardy seems to understand man's erotic impulse (what in *Tess* he calls the "inherent will to enjoy"), there is so little for many of his characters to enjoy that their attachment to life becomes tenuous, their vulnerability to the death instinct inevitable.

That so many of his major characters are unwilling to endure their suffering and, sooner or later, effect their own destruction did nothing to assuage the growing cultural anxieties of Hardy's later Victorian readers. But Hardy was too convinced of the artistic truth of what he wrote to be reasoned, badgered, or intimidated out of his "disagreeable" views. He believed that art is a disproportioning of realities, to show more clearly the feature in them which appeals most strongly to the idiosyncrasy of the artist. And the novelist's chief purpose in writing, he claimed, is to fascinate, like the Ancient Mariner, and "give pleasure by gratifying the love of the uncommon in human experience, mental or corporeal" (*L*, pp. 225–29, 150). Suicide, like the other catastrophes in Hardy's fiction, is employed to illustrate his temper and create artistic pleasure.

It is obvious that Hardy often overestimated his reader's tolerance for the uncommon, but his own fascination, particularly for violent forms of the uncommon, persisted all his life. In his "ghosted" autobiography (a strange book which substitutes for a narrative line a nonfictional series of seemings, personal impressions, anecdotes, portions of letters, notes on art and travel and social engagements), Hardy records a great many incidents which, taken together, help us better understand the formation of his idiosyncratic imagination and account for the pervasiveness of self-destructiveness in his art. For all its miscellaneous character, patterns emerge—clusters of entries that provide a basis for seeing Hardy clear, albeit not whole—and despite recent discussion about the omissions, distortions, and slantings of the *Life*, it remains an indispensable repository of information about Hardy's youthful experiences and emotions.[7] There is enough of what he encountered and felt to acquaint us with the kinds of materials and feelings which inform his art. And this, I suspect, is all we can expect from a reclusive Victorian who felt that all posterity needs to know of an author's life is what he wrote.

One very important group of entries deals with the violence and brutality of life in the country. Hardy reports having seen men placed in the stocks for punishment and he records his feelings at the burning of effigies of the Pope and Cardinal Wiseman. Robert Gittings gives an excellent account of demonstrations, riots, and whippings in Hardy's early life. Closer to home, Gittings relates tales of drunkenness, wife beating, and family rivalries under the roofs of Hardy's uncles and aunts, where he spent a good deal of time in his formative years (*YH*, pp. 14–15, 21–23). Local traditions associated with the Tolpuddle Martyrs and the bloody Hanging Judge Jeffreys were available, and poverty and starvation were widespread in the country in the first two decades of Hardy's life. His childish sympathy for repeal of the Corn Laws is expressed by his brandishing a toy sword, which was dipped in the blood of a newly killed pig, and exclaiming, "Free trade or blood!" (*L*, p. 21). Both his mother and grandmother had tales of personal poverty and suffering to share with the boy, who naturally adopted his mother's somber view of fate. And two savage tales, one told by his father, the other by his mother, seem to have had a deep and abiding influence on "the morbidly sensitive boy," as Gittings calls him (*YH*, p. 18). The father's tale was about the hanging of four men, the mother's about a youthful girl's suicide and horrible burial.

Hardy's emotional and psychological orientation was reinforced by his youthful reading in the world's finest literature of violence, suffering, and self-destruction: the Old Testament, Greek tragedy, Shakespeare, and the traditional ballads. Characteristically, he never forgot the ballad "The Outlandish Knight," which he first heard at a harvest supper. It includes the stanza he quoted in *Life* (p. 20):

> Lie there, lie there, thou false-hearted man,
> Lie there instead o' me;
> For six pretty maidens thou hast a-drown'd here,
> But the seventh hath drown-ed thee!

Nor could the revolutionary romanticism of his beloved Shelley, especially his advocacy of emotional freedom and his prophecy of the triumph of love, counter the effects of such a program of study upon such a temperament as Hardy's. Ironically, Hardy's fictional presentations of the futility of one's quest for freedom and the failure of love often end in the despair and loneliness that cause his protagonists to destroy themselves.

Clearly, the most dramatic events for the youthful Hardy were the two hangings he witnessed, both of which he remembered all his life (*L*, pp. 28–29). In his typically unselfconscious manner, Hardy remarks that the "unusual incident" of a hanging is reported because of its dramatic interest, even "though it had nothing to do with his own life"! The second Mrs. Hardy, however, felt that his attendance "may have given a tinge of bitterness and gloom to his life's work." Examining the youth's sensations after the hangings, Gittings offers his judgment of "perverse morbidity" in Hardy (*YH*, pp. 32–35).

An event of singular momentousness for the development of Hardy's temperament is hardly treated in the *Life*. This is the suicide of Horace Moule, typified in the poetry as "my friend"—the young and brilliant classical scholar who guided and encouraged Hardy's early studies and prose efforts. Gittings gives the most convincing account of Moule's impact on Hardy, who in adolescence was particularly susceptible to Moule's winning personality and responsive to his tutorial skills. Hardy's skeptical, critical turn of mind was fostered by Moule and the magazine to which he introduced Hardy in 1857, the *Saturday Review*. Though it is impossible to estimate exactly the effects of Moule's depressive nature and suicide upon Hardy, Gittings' final assessment demands serious consideration.

> The certainty is that, from the time of the death of Moule, Hardy never portrayed a man who was not, in some way, maimed by fate. He did not hesitate to load the dice at every point against his tragic heroes. Even if a case can be made that their own weakness or foolishness or rashness of choice caused their downfall, Hardy also made sure that the results would be as dire as possible by

introducing other elements of coincidence, irony, and what seems like divine indifference or even malevolence. He does this with absolute conviction, because, he is now fully persuaded, such things do occur, in all their extremes, in real life. However much his naturally sombre mind inclined that way before, however much his own identification with Job and the prophets of destruction may have coloured his expression, we can date the emergence of Hardy as a fully tragic artist, an expounder of man's true miseries, from the suicide of his friend, and the appalling revealed ironies of that personal history. [*YH*, p. 186]

After Moule's death, Hardy double-marked the two lines from Tennyson's *In Memoriam:* "Diffused the shock thro' all my life, / But in the present broke the blow."[8]

The effects of the shock are evident throughout his fictional career, as Hardy's imagination greedily, almost compulsively, sought to represent his impressions of life's frailty. As one of his duties as a practicing novelist, Hardy filled a number of notebooks with accounts from magazines and newspapers of violent and sensational events, and not infrequently, such events underwent imaginative metamorphosis and later were incorporated into Hardy's fictions.

In his unpublished "Facts" notebook are many entries from the "Accidents and Offences" column of the *Dorset County Chronicle,* the local newspaper, whose files Hardy apparently worked through in the early 1880s.[9] Drownings, rick burnings, shipwrecks, robberies, poisonings, murders: such were the staples of this column, and many such events find their way into Hardy's notebook. So too do more bizarre occurrences, such as the selling of wives and the drinking binge of a man who had vowed for many years not to take any liquor. Hardy's use of this kind of "fact" in *The Mayor of Casterbridge* illustrates his commitment to the real and true, particularly when the real possesses the attractions of the violent and uncommon.

In his notebook are no fewer than twenty-five entries on suicides, a good many taken from the pages of the *Dorset County Chronicle* in the 1820s. Hardy preserved accounts of young girls who committed suicide after being separated from their lovers or scolded by their fathers. There are men who destroy themselves after drinking bouts, gambling losses, in remorse at the death of a wife, and shock at frustration of long-expected hopes for provision in old age. A child of ten took her life when her father humiliated her by ordering her to wear her everyday clothes on a Sunday. A lad of fourteen, a steady apprentice in surgery, drowned himself after he had begun to associate with improper females of the town. A rector hanged himself by the bell rope in the church's belfry; a prostitute drowned herself after the death of her brawling lover; a pair of French lovers shot each other in the heart amid the merrymaking of a wedding. In an entry on the great distress and poverty in the country, three consequences were noted: suicides, horse stealing, and highway robberies. In some cases of suicide, no apparent motive, no reason, was assigned for the act; in others, juries or coroners brought in verdicts of insanity or momentary derangement. Hardy noted the tradition of a late-night, crossroad burial for suicides in an unblest grave; there was no religious service, no coffin, and a stake was driven through the suicides' bodies.

The large number of such entries, it seems, convinced Hardy that suicide is hardly uncommon and that all kinds of people, even the very young, are vulnerable. Though there is little appropriation of these newspaper accounts directly into Hardy's novels,[10] he absorbed the evidence of human vulnerability to wrecked love affairs, to the pain of humiliation, to the frustration of hope; and he educated himself to understand that what appears to be the most trivial of acts, such as a father's thoughtless scolding of his child or a weekend binge, can lead the person to destroy himself. From the strictly technical point of view, the notebook entries substantiate a "fact" that develops into a pervasive theme in Hardy's novels. Self-destruction is appropriated, in its manifold forms, among Hardy's imaginative raw materials; it is available as accompaniment to or the culmination of catastrophe in a tragedy. Hardy could "use" suicide just as he "used Jude's difficulties of study" or as he might have "used" war, fire, or shipwreck.[11]

Hardy's fascination with self-destruction also commands attention for what it reveals about his personal nature. From the time of his birth—when he was literally cast aside as dead and survived only because of the midwife's alertness—Hardy had cause to be concerned about his physical feebleness and his power to endure life. Millgate reports that the infant was "so lacking in motion and discernible intelligence" that his mother soon was convinced she had borne an idiot, and family tradition suggests that Hardy's parents, fearing the weakly child was unlikely to live, took little interest in him, or feared to make any great emotional commitment to him.[12] Jemima Hardy's subsequent overprotectiveness only reinforced the child's sense of frailty and emotional insecurity. Thus his imaginative and actual encounters with violence and suffering were powerful agents, intensifying his sensitivity to the fragility of human life and man's vulnerability to the aggressiveness in his fellow humans and in nature. Moreover, his almost instinctive anxiety about Change and Time, the legacy of Jemima's terrifying fatalism, accounts for Hardy's precocious desire, in his personal life, to withdraw from experience, to resist new acquaintances, to refuse the risks of hope.

That foreboding incident early in the *Life*, where Hardy lies on his back, looking through his straw hat at the sun, is a poignant intimation of the strain of melancholy that permeates many of his works (*L*, pp. 15–16). Deeply sensitive to how useless he was and alert to the sufferings of the physically frail, Hardy concluded that he did not wish to grow up, or leave home, or meet new people. Still, much more is apparent in the incident than what Hardy points to—namely, his lack of social ambition. The feeling of personal worthlessness intermittently dogged "Thomas the Unworthy" (as he called himself) throughout his life (*L*, p. 200), and such excessive denigration of the self accounts for the tenuous attachment to life we recognize in Henchard and Tess and Jude, who succumb to self-destructiveness when they cannot allay their feelings of unworthiness and guilt.

Hardy's hope to retreat from life's suffering and his desire, as a boy, to elude change by stopping time are fairly common, quite normal emotions; for a child whose ambitious mother pushed him to the limits of his physical and social nature, they are readily comprehensible. Moreover, there is a conventional literary note in this scene (which, after all, was written by the much older ex-novelist) which derives from and suggests the degree to which Hardy's emotional nature was formed by reading the poetry of his favorites, Wordsworth, Shelley, Keats, and Browning. In the young Hardy's wish to avoid change we detect a Romantic "quest for permanence" or, as Browning calls it, a yearning to retain the "infinite moment," wherein Time is halted and the emotions of the "golden instant" are sealed and preserved from Time's altering march. But what distinguished Hardy's youthful quest for permanence—what gave it a noxious, subversive cast—was precisely his sense of unworthiness; and his desire *not* to grow was not only unrealistic and immature, it was, more insidiously, rejection of a self which often seemed unfit for the struggle for survival and without sufficient self-esteem to face Time squarely. It was virtually rejection of his life. Hardy wrote of that desperate phase in "For Life I Had Never Cared Greatly."[13]

If this incident were unique, it would have little interest for us, but early in life Hardy reflected on a world that neglects us (L, p. 83), a world full of "agony, darkness, death also" (L, p. 112). He often questioned whether he had staying power to hold his own in the world and in literature, and even questioned, only days before his death, if his work had been worth doing (L, p. 444). Subject to lengthy bouts with depression and permanently scarred by disappointed hopes and feelings of insecurity and guilt, especially over his insensitivity to his first wife's suffering, Hardy instinctively recognized and sympathized with those desperate alter egos he seems to perceive everywhere. On March 5, 1890, for example, he saw a "staid, worn, weak man at the railway station. His back, his legs, his hands, his face, were longing to be out of the world" (L, p. 224). Few authors have understood this longing as well as Hardy, so many of whose works are informed by the "skull beneath the skin" theme. In the poem "Tess's Lament," the narrator speaks for a good number of Hardy's major fictional characters when she says:

> I cannot bear my fate as writ,
>   I'd have my life unbe;
> Would turn my memory to a blot,
> Make every relic of me rot,
> My doings be as they were not,
>   And gone all trace of me! [CP, #141]

"I'd have my life unbe"! Hardy seems often to have shared this wish with Tess. The earliest occasion when he recorded the wish that he were dead was after he read a review of *Desperate Remedies* in the *Spectator* (L, p. 84). Many another author has expressed the same sentiment upon seeing his first novel panned, I feel certain, but there were many evenings, Hardy confided to his friend Edmund Gosse, when he had gone to bed hoping never to see daylight again.[14] Also, there are several personal poems in which the same wish is uttered, though none is so searing as the "*In Tenebris*" sequence, with its epigraphs from Psalms (*CP,* #136–38). The motto of the first of this trio may be translated, "My heart is smitten, and withered like grass," and in the second's motto are the phrases "there was no man that would know me . . . no man cared for my soul." The smitten heart and the alienated, unloved soul of the first pair of poems lead the narrator to reflect, in the motto of the third poem, "Alas, that my stay is prolonged . . . my soul has been long away from home." This serenely lucid and stoical poem begins:

> There have been times when I well might have passed and the
>   ending have come—
> Points in my path when the dark might have stolen on me,
>   artless, unrueing—
> Ere I had learnt that the world was a welter of futile doing:
> Such had been times when I well might have passed, and the
>   ending have come!

How often, after Emma's death, had Hardy imagined his life's ending? In "The Prospect," a poem that recalls (for me) Tennyson's strategy in "Break, Break, Break," of contrasting the emotions of the bereaved lover with the vital playfulness of the young, Hardy's "merry boys go forth to look for slides" while the desperately lonely Hardy moans, "But well, well do I know / Whither I would go!" (*CP,* #735).

Hardy records a conversation in his autobiography in which he and Lady Catherine Milnes-Gaskell "talked of suicide, pessimism, whether life was worth living, and kindred dismal subjects." We can infer the nature of their conclusions when he tells us that, at the end of their discussion, they "were quite miserable" (*L*, p. 259). That Hardy may actually have relished this conversation should not surprise us—did he not take impish delight in pointing out to friends places where suicides often occurred?[15] And did he not work cheerfully, year after year, at composing what Florence Hardy considered dreadfully morbid poems? An undeniable gothic strain in Hardy's nature led him to play with the terrible realities of suffering and death; still, we should not underestimate the seriousness of his preoccupation with suicide. For him, the desire never to have been born was far more than a traditional poetic trope, while the wish to have his life "unbe" seems to have recurred often and been very powerful at certain stages. His self-destructive characters are drawn from deep within his own experience, as Hardy's spring of vitality, never overflowing, seems early to have run dry.

Another explanation for Hardy's repeated use of self-destruction also deserves consideration. However we may wish to characterize his preoccupation with violent death and suicide (*pace*, Harrison and Gittings; I consider Hardy one of the most human, perceptive, courageously outspoken, and healthy of authors),[16] and whatever weight we give his technical use of suicide for his fictional effects, we cannot overlook what might be called Hardy's "artistic creed" and "prophetic mission." Like many of his eminent predecessors, Hardy sometimes conceived of himself as a latter-day prophet, crying out in the wilderness of modern life to a threatened community. I think of him as an "intellectual deliverer," in the sense Matthew Arnold meant in his essay "The Modern Element in Literature": one who contemplates and communicates the spirit of the age.[17]

A skeptic by temperament, Hardy early learned to admire the liberated intellectualism of Milton, Gibbon,

Shelley, and John Stuart Mill. His critical bent took shape under the tutelage of Horace Moule and the social protestations of the conservative *Saturday Review*, and in his early days in London he received with enthusiasm what many of his contemporaries felt were the "subversive" works of Darwin, Huxley, Swinburne, and the authors of *Essays and Reviews*. Hardy's instincts and his reading, it seems clear, equipped him to welcome the awakening of the modern spirit. To act as a "dissolvent" of the "old European system of dominant ideas & facts" is, from the planning of *The Poor Man and the Lady* to the publication of *Jude the Obscure*, one of Hardy's most enduring artistic aims, and his method is related to that of Goethe, "that grand dissolvent" whom Arnold considered Europe's sagest head. Goethe advises that "man must live from within outwards, so the artist must work from within outwards, seeing that, make what contortions he will, he can only bring to light his own individuality."[18] However quaintly he expressed it, Hardy's instinct for elaborating his "idiosyncratic mode of regard" seems to share eminently reputable critical kinship with Goethe's thought.

But Hardy would be more than a "dissolvent"; he would be a prophet too. He wrote to Mrs. Henniker that "if you mean to make the world listen to you, you must say now what they will all be thinking and saying five and twenty years hence: and if you do that you must offend your conventional friends."[19] Hardy never lost much sleep over fear of offending the conventional; a shaper of such stuff as dreams are made on, he believed, must disregard what is customary and apply himself to the real function of art: the application of ideas to life.[20] But to express his "seemings" or impressions fully and sincerely, the artist must be freed from the constraints of publishers and reviewers. Nothing disgusted Hardy more than the insincerity of much of contemporary literature, but this was to be expected when the standard for publication in magazines was whether the subject could bring a blush to the cheeks of adolescent females. Hardy's most impassioned plea for artistic and intellectual liberty is "Candour in English Fiction," where he calls for a "sincere school of Fiction," one which "expresses truly the views prevalent in its time" (*PW*, p. 126). Hardy argued that "untrammelled adult opinion on conduct and theology" might be dramatically appealed to; he hoped that "the position of man and woman in nature, and the position of belief in the minds of man and woman—things which everybody is thinking but nobody is saying—might be taken up and treated frankly."

Though "conduct and theology" are always at issue in Hardy's fiction, and are treated in the context of sexual and marital relations, the impossibility of fully developing his materials plagued him to the end of his career, even after he had established himself as the greatest living English novelist. In 1890 Hardy believed (wrongly, he was to learn) that the literary climate favored the kind of intellectual deliverance for which he felt suited; he sensed "a revival of the artistic instincts towards great dramatic motives," as worked out by the Periclean and Elizabethan dramatists and, on the contemporary stage, by the Norwegian Henrik Ibsen. Attempting to vindicate the tone and form of his fictions, Hardy wrote: "Differing natures find their tongue in the presence of differing spectacles. Some natures become vocal at tragedy, some are made vocal by comedy, and it seems to me that to whichever of these aspects of life a writer's instinct for expression the more readily responds, to that he should allow it to respond" (*PW*, p. 49).

To the evolution of high tragedy in his time, Hardy hoped to contribute "further truths—in other words, original treatment": "treatment which seeks to show Nature's unconsciousness not of essential laws, but of those laws framed merely as social expedients by humanity, without a basis in the heart of things; treatment which expresses the triumph of the crowd over the hero, of the commonplace majority over the exceptional few" (*PW*, p. 127).

In his last, most modern novels, Hardy was committed to a view of life as "a physiological fact, [and] its honest portrayal must be largely concerned with, for one thing, the relation of the sexes" (*PW*, p. 127). But affronted by the adverse critical reception of his finest and most important works, Hardy could not preserve Goethe's Olympian politeness. In preface after preface he pointed out that there is more to be said about imprudent marriages, a young girl's loss of virginity, and the deadly war waged between flesh and spirit, and he would have his say "without a mincing of words." His catastrophes would be "based upon sexual relations as it is [*sic*]," despite the well-nigh insuperable bar imposed by English society. And without flinching, he would show in his works on love and death the costs in pain and suffering—no matter how extreme—paid by his poor puppets.

CHAPTER TWO

Changing Views on Suicide

IN HARDY'S EFFORTS to "spread over art the latest
illumination of the time" and "intensify the expression of
things," he often permitted his characters the opportunity
to destroy themselves. Suicide, as a matter of fact, was
among the modern subjects which many were thinking
about but few were speaking of. In the aftermath of the
French Revolution, Romantic Wertherism, and Byronism,
the cultural mood throughout Europe may be depicted as "a
drift from unrest to an intense excitement, from excitement
to bewilderment, and hence to a darkening disillusionment."[1] This steady drift, which left its mark on the major
creative artists, intellectuals, and scientists, is reflected in
their growing awareness of and concern over the rising
number of suicides. In particular, the widespread notion
that, by century's end, man had lost his vitality—had become hypersensitive and effete—bespeaks a malaise and
loss of hope that imparts a tragic tone to much of the
literature of the last two decades of the Victorian era. From
the disillusionment of Matthew Arnold's narrator in
"Stanzas from the Grande Chartreuse" to the despair of his

hero in *Empedocles on Etna* is not a long journey, and these mid-Victorian poems anticipate a crucial later-Victorian spiritual crisis and chart a course which is to be followed throughout the century. Inevitably, it leads one step beyond what human sensibility can bear. Oscar Wilde, whose personal career seems to epitomize the *fin de siécle* movement from intensity to disillusionment and despair, strikes the note of sadness and intimates man's self-destructiveness in "Humanitad":

> Ah! it was easy when the world was young
>   To keep one's life free and inviolate,
> From our sad lips another song is rung,
>   By our own hands our heads are desecrate.

In the speculation and literature of the time, one question keeps being asked: Is life worth living? And increasingly, in life as well as in art, two desperate responses recurred: Would that I had never been born! and I wish that I were dead. Readers of Hardy's novels hear these responses as leitmotifs.

As artists and intellectuals became aware of the increasing incidence of self-destruction, the popular assumption that suicide was a specifically French form of madness was giving way to more informed judgments. Some of the extra-literary findings during Hardy's lifetime suggest an evolving context of discussions and theorizing in relation to which his fictions may be read. The insightful perspectives and precise vocabulary developed by social scientists, moreover, are useful in illuminating the social and psychological pressures that contributed to Hardy's characters' suicides. Typically, Hardy's impressions about suicide departed from the conventional Victorian view and, impressively but not surprisingly, anticipated some of the most authoritative theories.

From 1840 through 1938, which corresponds fairly closely to Hardy's life, the subject of human self-destructiveness challenged the minds and hearts and stimulated the inquiries of physicians, historians, sociologists, psychoanalysts, and creative artists. The most notable efforts were the moralistic Christian assessment of Dr. Forbes Winslow (the scholarly contrast of pagan and Christian ethics of suicide), the rigorous but imaginatively scientific social determinism of Emile Durkheim, and the brilliant psychoanalytical theorizing initiated by Sigmund Freud and continued by Karl Menninger. The application of these various ways of knowing indicates an important phase of the movement of mind in the period and suggests the extent of the inquiry into a disturbing modern phenomenon. The impressions and theories that resulted were formulated as responses to roughly the same disrupted, confusing, and alienating world into which Hardy was born and which he reflects in his fiction. Though much of the scientific literature was produced abroad and remained untranslated (or even unpublished) during Hardy's career as novelist and, therefore, was unavailable to him (in the sense of a direct influence), it is considered here because, in documenting in intellectual terms the lived experiences and feelings of many European contemporaries of Hardy, it enables us more fully to understand Hardy's sensitivity to a crucial issue of his time and to appreciate the artistic precision with which he drew his many tragic portraits of suicides.

In 1840 Dr. Forbes Winslow, a member of the Royal College of Surgeons in London, wrote *The Anatomy of Suicide*, the first study in England devoted exclusively to such an inquiry in moral philosophy. Because of Winslow's learned approach and thorough treatment and because his book represents the thought of a conventional Victorian Christian at the time of Hardy's birth, it is particularly valuable for re-creating the intellectual and emotional atmosphere in which suicide was discussed—the background against which many of Hardy's impressions are opposed.

As a doctor, Winslow considered suicide in reference to its physiological and pathological character. He tried to establish the "fact of primary importance," that suicide often originates in derangement of the brain and abdominal viscera, and he wished to disprove the opinion that those who commit suicide in apparent coolness are in possession of a sound mind.[2] But Winslow's approach was by no means narrowly specialized, in our modern sense. An advocate of "mental philosophy" or psychology, Winslow traced "the reciprocity of action existing between different mental conditions, and affections of particular organs." Since passions exercise such tyranny over the physical economy, Winslow believed it "natural to expect that the crime of suicide should be traced to the influence of mental causes" (AS, p. 49).

Winslow's moralistic bias emerges in his use of the word "crime," and he refused to grant any authority to the teaching or examples of ancient advocates of suicide, for "we live under a Christian dispensation. Our notions of death, of honour, and of courage, are, in many respects, so dissimilar from those which the ancients entertained, that the subject of suicide is placed on a different basis" (p. 2). Of the three "justifiable" causes of suicide in antiquity—avoidance of pain and suffering of body and mind, vindication of honor, and the sacrifice of one's life as an example for others— Winslow found the first cause most excusable, but ultimately he condemned "this recklessness of human life" among the ancients (p. 22). He summarily dismissed the thought of more recent advocates of suicide: "The arguments which have been advanced by Hume, Donne, Rousseau, Madame de Staël, Montesquieu, Montaigne, Gibbon,

Voltaire, and Robeck, are founded on such gross and apparent fallacies that they carry with them their own refutation." Dr. Winslow was fully serious, it seems, when he proclaimed physicians not inferior to *anyone* in knowledge of those higher branches of philosophy that dignify and elevate human character! (pp. v – vi).

The tenor of Winslow's thought is caught in his statement that "we are wise and good just in proportion as we consider and treat life and all its incidents as moral means to a great end." Discussing the differences in the lot of men, he insisted that

> some experience pleasure, others pain, privation or suffering; the tools with which we are to work may be inconvenient or burthensome, or light and pleasant; but they must be the most useful and efficacious, or they would not be put into our hands; at any rate, they are all we have. We cannot fix too deeply on our minds the truth that life is not an absolute, but a relative existence, as in its relation to the eternity with which it is connected, consists all its value and importance. [p. 40]

If Winslow sounds more like a preacher than a physician, if his tone is more polemical than scientific, it is because he was committed to a Christian view of suicide. Using biblical quotations and theological reasoning—even refuting Paley on this issue of moral philosophy—Winslow asserted that suicide is "forbidden as a *sin*, which it is only in the power of God to take cognizance of, in another world" (p. 37; Winslow's italics).

Winslow was in fuller accord with other observers of society when he theorized that suicide increases with the level of refinement and civilization. He attributed the increase in suicides in England in the mid-nineteenth century to chronic political excitement, "to a certain extent to be traced to the atrocious doctrines promulgated with such zeal by the sect of modern infidels, who falsely denominate themselves *Socialists;* a class whose opinions are subversive of all morality and Christianity, and which sap the foundation of society itself." The ideas of Robert Owen and works like Goethe's *Werther* are to be repudiated, Winslow argued, by sound-thinking Christians (pp. 82–85, 93).

Winslow acknowledged a number of physical causes of suicide,[3] primarily visceral derangement, leading to melancholia and hypochondriasis (Eustacia Vye's most common complaints). And for Winslow, the hereditary character of suicide was a clearly established fact. But Winslow marshaled his rhetoric to assert that, whatever the physical disturbances in the system, "the brain, and the brain alone, is the seat of the disease in all cases of suicide" (p. 220).

Of the "passions of the mind," none so readily drives a person to suicide as remorse. Winslow also discussed the effects upon a suicidal disposition of guilt, unrequited and irregulated love, jealousy, mortified pride, despair, dread of poverty and want, aspirations too high and disappointed ambitions, the loss of dear ones, and sudden reverses of fortune. But for all his awareness of human miseries, physical and mental, and although he acknowledged in the human mind a "natural propensity" to destroy, "even the most impassioned desire to kill others or oneself," Winslow concluded with Dr. Rowley, whom he quoted without disapproval: "No rational being will voluntarily give himself pain, or deprive himself of life." Therefore, everyone who commits suicide "is indubitably *non compos mentis*" and "suicide should ever be considered an act of insanity" (pp. 222, 224).

If in 1840 Winslow seemed unwilling to give the ancients a fair hearing on self-destruction and if he was convinced of the cowardliness, sinfulness, criminality, and insanity of the suicide, his positions were subject to reconsideration by the last quarter of the century, particularly as a result of the renewed interest in paganism created by (among other things) the poetry of Swinburne, the essays of Matthew Arnold and Walter Pater, and the *History of European Morals from Augustus to Charlemagne*, written in 1869 by W. E. H. Lecky. In his published literary notebook, Hardy entered a number of passages from "The Ethics of Suicide," an article that drew much of its substance from Lecky and appeared in the *Saturday Review* for June 17, 1876. Given his lifelong interest in the culture and art of ancient times, it is not surprising that Hardy clipped the piece and took artistic nourishment from it at the time he was working on *The Return of the Native*.[4]

Hardy's notebook entries emphasize the Stoic's ideal of virtue, based on a self-complacent faith in human perfection and dignity. As the Stoics recognized no responsibility to a Higher Power, they felt no guilt at offending him, no fear of a future judgment. "The worldly code of respectability & honour . . . was held synonymous with the highest virtue" (*LN*, pp. 1, 48). The arguments of the great Roman writers, moreover, are cited in support of suicide. In three proximate entries, Hardy noted Marcus Aurelius' idea that man may be duty bound to take his life as a means of escaping the risk of moral deterioration, Seneca's advocacy of suicide as a refuge to the oppressed and suffering, and Pliny's belief that man is happy in possessing a resource denied to the immortal gods, that is, suicide.

Though Winslow argued that Cato chose suicide in cowardly insanity, "The Ethics of Suicide" praises his act as "the culminating point of the Stoic system, which held out no hope of immortal joys, taught men to despise all fear of death." Cato's choice arose "out of a deification of human pride, which shrank from humiliation, cherished no sense of sin, & acknowledged no duty of obedience to a superior will" (*LN*, pp. 1, 49). In none of Hardy's entries is there any question of the sinfulness, criminality, or insanity of the suicide, nor does Hardy (in his parenthetical markings) raise such issues. Strictly speaking, in the context of pagan ethics such questions are irrelevant or wrongheaded; and in Hardy's fictions, those who commit suicide are often motivated by the pagan values represented in this essay. In the cases of Farmer Boldwood and Tess, who find themselves in the unfortunate situation of being pagans in a post-Christian world, the social and legal judgments of their criminality and insanity are hardly the novels' final word. (These figures will be considered more fully in their appropriate places.)

The book by Dr. Winslow and the essay in the *Saturday Review* are just two of numerous studies of suicide written in Europe during the 1800s. As doctors, psychologists, and sociologists took up the subject in the last two centuries, the question of the rightness or wrongness of suicide began to yield to the problem of its causes. In 1897, at the end of Hardy's career as a novelist, Emile Durkheim's monumental *Le Suicide* appeared, culminating the century's energetic study of the subject and documenting with imaginative brilliance (in his use and interpretation of statistics) the development of suicidal tendencies in revolution-ridden European societies. Durkheim's definitions, typology, and complex perception of the interconnectedness of suicide with social and natural phenomena are not only indispensable for any study of the subject, but his having written, in 1897, such a brilliant analysis of the contemporary social context, which Hardy reflects in his fiction, makes Durkheim peculiarly relevant for an analysis of the modernity and authenticity of Hardy's impressions about suicide.

Durkheim catalogued the era's most familiar suicidal types and intimated the chief cause of the rise in the suicide rate:

The anarchist, the aesthete, the mystic, the socialist revolutionary, even if they do not despair of the future, have in common with the pessimist a single sentiment of hatred and disgust for the existing order, a single craving to destroy or to escape from reality. Collective melancholy would not have penetrated consciousness so far, if it had not undergone a morbid development; and so the development of suicide resulting from it is of the same nature.[5]

Durkheim's diagnosis evokes such representative Victorians as Wilde, Pater, Arnold, Clough, Tennyson, Ruskin, and Housman—all disturbed by the "collective melancholy," and some victimized by it.

The concept of collective melancholy is an instance of Durkheim's "collective representations," which, in a given society, constitute the "collective consciousness." These representations exist outside the individual consciousness, on which they operate coercively. They are determined directly—not through the thoughts and emotions of individuals, but in permanent expressions and written law, works of art, literature, and statistical averages. The collective representations operate in ways suggestive of Hardy's idea of an "Immanent Will," although Hardy gives greater emphasis to man's "physical" bondage.

Man's privilege is that the bond he accepts is not physical but moral; that is, social. He is governed not by a material environment brutally imposed on him, but by a conscience superior to his own, the superiority of which he feels. Because the greater, better part of his existence transcends the body, he escapes the body's yoke, but is subject to that of society.

But when society is disturbed by some painful crisis or by beneficent but abrupt transitions, it is momentarily incapable of exercising this influence; thus come the sudden rises in the curves of suicides. [S, p. 252]

Durkheim regards suicide statistics as a social fact which expresses the suicidal tendency of a society. A society's suicide rate changes if the character of the society alters; and the number of suicides depends on the extent of an individual's integration with the social group—the family, professional organization, religious community—and varies inversely with the degree of integration of the social groups of which the individual forms a part. According to Durkheim, the bond that attaches people to life relaxes because the bond that attaches them to society is slack. The events of private life, which seem to some observers a direct inspiration of suicide and are considered determining causes, are in reality only incidental causes. The individual yields to the slightest shock of circumstance because the state of society has made the person a ready prey to suicide (p. 215).

In his definition of suicide, Durkheim attempted to comprehend all forms of self-destruction, even those which normally go unacknowledged by the common man and unreported in statistics. He applied the term "suicide" to "any death which is the direct or indirect result of a positive or negative act accomplished by the victim himself." Durkheim's examples are instructive in illustrating the variety of suicidal types: refusal to take food is equivalent to self-destruction by a dagger or firearm; the iconoclast, who knowingly commits a capital crime and dies by the executioner's hand, achieves his own death as truly as though he had dealt his own death blow; the soldier, facing certain death, who tries to save his regiment; the martyr, dying for his faith; the mother, sacrificing herself for her child. "Thus, when resolution entails certain sacrifice of life, scientifically this is suicide" (pp. 42–44).

In dealing with motivation, Durkheim asked, "Should suicide exist only if the act resulting in death was performed to gain that end? Should suicide be nothing more than intentional self-homicide?" He answered in the negative, because motives are often unrecognizable or misjudged, even escaping the observation of the suicide himself. Moreover, people feel genuine reluctance to face up to and admit a suicide, even when it is obvious.[6] Those who kill themselves "by accident," as well as those who sustain serious injuries during an attempt to commit suicide and die weeks or months later of these injuries or recurrent infections, are never registered as suicides, although Durkheim considered them as such.

Since Durkheim's explanation for suicide was sociological, the presumed causes were also defined that way, and the three major types of suicide— "egoistic," "altruistic," and "anomic"—result from the degree of integration and regulation of the individual's social existence. Thus *egoism, altruism,* and *anomie* identify states of groups or social conditions that cause people to commit suicide. (Durkheim warned, however, that differentiating too rigidly between types is difficult; for example, suicides are sometimes of an egoistic-anomic character.)

The degree of integration within society determines the types of suicide.[7] Examining religious, familial, and political society, Durkheim found "egoistic suicide," which results from the individual's lack of involvement in and concern with society, widespread in Europe in the nineteenth century. Because in egoistic societies feelings, beliefs, values, and traditions are pluralistic, collective life declines and individualism asserts itself. With the individual's removal from the control of the group, society's prophylactic influence is reduced: collective beliefs cannot withstand the corrosive effects of free inquiry, collective sentiments decline as the number of family relationships dwindles, and dissociation from the body politic isolates the individual from the "common causes" that unite society. With decline of the insulating, integrating effects of such collective be-

liefs, sentiments, and activities, the individual soon finds
life to be meaningless and intolerably burdensome. The
egoistic suicide is often characterized by depression and
apathy, produced by exaggerated individuation (p. 356).

Just as *lack* of integration leads to higher suicide rates, so
does *excessive* integration. When the individual is totally
wrapped up in and controlled by society, his individuality is
so slightly developed that it cannot be highly valued. Society does not hesitate to send the individual to death, nor
does the individual resist the command to end the existence
which he himself finds of small worth. Suicides of this sort
(called "altruistic") are "obligatory" when society compels
them, with the threat of punishment or dishonor, and "op-
tional" when society merely counsels them as avenues to
honors and postlife rewards. Primitive society and military
society revealed to Durkheim the spirit of renunciation and
abnegation that is characteristic of altruistic suicides. The
altruist commits suicide because he finds little meaning in
continuing physical existence or because he locates it in a
life beyond the present one; the egoist does so because he
fails to fulfill his need to find life's meaning. In both instances, the lack of meaning is decisive.

Durkheim's third type, "anomic suicide," results when
major disruptions in the social organism reduce society's
regulatory influence on the individual. Durkheim reasoned
that the individual's needs and their satisfaction have been
regulated by society; the common beliefs and practices he
has learned make him the embodiment of the "collective
conscience." But when social regulation is upset, as in times
of economic crises or because of divorce, the individual's
horizon is contracted unduly or broadened beyond what he
can endure. Often the need to reduce one's requirements,
restrain one's passions, and learn self-control becomes intolerable and begets exasperation, which turns the individual

against the self or others (pp. 252–53). Typically, the anomic suicide goes to death in anger and disappointment, full of violent recriminations against life in general or a particular person who has ruined his life (p. 284).

Suicide, like crime, is for Durkheim no indication of immorality in itself. Actually, a given number of suicides is to be expected in a given type of society; but when the rate increases inordinately, it signals the breakdown of the collective conscience and the appearance of a basic flaw in the social fabric. Suicide and criminality are not correlative, as some moralists and criminologists had claimed; but when both are excessive, it indicates that the social structure is not functioning normally (pp. 16–17).

Durkheim's sociological approach, while it recognizes that suicide appears to be a personal matter, insists that it can only be explained in terms of the state of the society to which an individual belongs. But the modern study of self-destruction is given impetus and a new direction by the research of psychologists and psychoanalysts who have sought the answer to the riddle of suicide by looking into man's mental state. The work begun by such European Victorians complements Durkheim's social determinism and reveals that self-destructive behavior is a combination of psycho-instinctual impulse and social precipitation.

The earliest notable contribution of the new analysts of the mind occurred in 1910, when the Vienna Psychoanalytic Society met to consider the "epidemic" of suicides among high school pupils. The ambitious inquiry, however, though conducted by some of the ablest professionals in the burgeoning field, did not yield the desired results. Sigmund Freud, the society's chairman and organizer of the symposium, admitted at the end of the session that no clear light was cast on the main problem of how the powerful life-preserving instinct is overcome. Still, some significant foun-

34 CHANGING VIEWS ON SUICIDE

dations, which served as a basis for further study, were laid. Alfred Adler saw suicide, like neurosis, as a "childish form of reaction to a childish overestimation of motivations, humiliations, and disappointments. It represents, like neurosis and psychosis, an escape by anti-social means from the injustices of life." Isidor Sadger claimed that "nobody commits suicide who has not given up hope for love." And Wilhelm Stekel said that "no one kills himself who did not want to kill another or, at least, wish death to another."[8]

Over the next two decades, Freud elaborated his concept of a "death instinct," locked in ceaseless struggle with the instinct of self-preservation (the archetypal conflict between Eros and Thanatos). Freud's complicated explanation of suicide as transposed murder formed the basis for later refinements about the psychic energy needed for self-destruction.[9] The theory was given its fullest elaboration in 1938, when Dr. Karl A. Menninger applied Freud's concept of the death instinct to the study of suicide (in his book *Man against Himself*) and identified three components in the suicidal act: the wish to kill (aggression), the wish to be killed (submission), and the wish to die. Menninger acknowledged that these three, usually unconscious motives of suicide "are complicated by extraneous factors—social attitudes, familial patterns, community customs, and also by those distortions of reality incident to an incomplete personality development." Yet he insisted that neither these factors, nor heredity, suggestion, or maladjustments, can *explain* suicide, which is due to self-destructive tendencies "first appearing long before the consummation of the critical act."[10]

Menninger traces the origin of the wish to kill to primitive self-destructiveness. It sometimes happens that the aggressive and destructive impulses one directs against another are deflected back upon the self. For example, it is possible to regard one's body as not being part of oneself, just as it is possible to treat one's body as if it includes the body of someone else. The latter phenomenon, introjection, occurs when a lover figuratively carries his sweetheart inside him. Turning hostile feelings back upon the self may occur when the self is prevented from working out its aggression against another because of lack of opportunity, a severe conscience, or a strongly neutralizing affection. Through such means, introjection serves a psychological usefulness: any desired treatment of the other person can be carried out upon oneself. It is the well-known device called "kicking the cat," with oneself (one's own body) used as the cat (*M*, p. 33).

Menninger states that the wish to kill can be verified if the facts relating to a suicide show that (a) there is a reflection of the destructive tendencies upon the individual, so that the self is treated as though it were an external object; (b) if persons who are prone to suicide prove to be highly ambivalent in their object attachments, masking, with their conscious, positive attachments, large and scarcely mastered quantities of unconscious hostility; and (c) if such individuals' suicides are precipitated by sudden interruptions in object attachment (p. 32).

Menninger explains that the wish to be killed results from the activity of the conscience, particularly the *lex talionis* (the law of retaliation), which insists that the ego must suffer in direct proportion to its externally directed destructiveness (pp. 32 – 53). The demands of the conscience are so great and so inexorable that sometimes there is no placating them (this is particularly true with melancholiacs). An individual's sense of guilt may arise from other acts than outright aggression, for, in the unconscious, a *wish* to destroy is equivalent to actual destruction—insofar as it exposes the ego to punishment. This phenomenon of the conscience explains why melancholiacs rarely kill anyone but themselves, even though their driving motive is the wish to kill someone else (pp. 54–55). Menninger insists that this wish to kill is usually unconscious and is often disguised by a conscious attitude of love, protection, obedience.

About the third motive, the wish to die, Menninger is much more tentative. He believes there is evidence that some of the original, self-directed aggressiveness contributes to the wish to die, and this wish combines with the more sophisticated motives and impels the precipitant self-destruction. The wish to die is often obvious in mental sickness and especially in melancholia, where the patient, as Freud has written, "is brutally self-critical in describing himself as petty, egoistic, dishonest, lacking in independence"—whose sole aim has been "to hide the weaknesses of his own nature."[11] Michael Henchard's death note is a classic example of the melancholic egoist's will to obliterate all signs of his painful existence.

Extending Freud's hypothesis of a death instinct opposed to the life instinct, Menninger suggests that the destructive tendencies may be neutralized, in part or in full, by the erotic tendencies. When the self-destructive impulses are partially (but not completely) neutralized, many forms of the death instinct occur in which the individual commits "slow" suicide ("suicide by inches"), which Menninger calls chronic self-destruction. Such forms of behavior, resulting in self-injury, such as asceticism and martyrdom, neurotic invalidism, chronic bad luck, and "purposeful" accidents (by which an individual postpones death indefinitely, at a cost of suffering and impairment of normal functions), are equivalent to "partial" suicide, a living death.[12]

Finally, Menninger gives examples of what Freud called "somatic compliance," the biological acceptance of the instinctual tendencies as modified or directed by the psyche.

Psychoanalysts hypothesize that certain bodily infections become serious in just those cases where there are strongly active self-destructive tendencies. It is possible, they think, that the strength of the death instinct determines this biological acceptance of extraneous opportunities for self-destruction (pp. 78–79).

Even so cursory a review as just presented reveals something of the urgency and intellectual intensity with which physicians, philosophers, and social scientists engaged the frightening paradox of suicide. But, as is often the case, creative artists monitor and record important shifts in action, thought, and feeling before the intellectual historians and social scientists are aware that such changes have occurred. In the study of suicide, in fact, the writings of Durkheim and Freud suggest that imaginative literature is nearly as important a form of evidence as mortuary statistics and case studies. And the reason seems obvious: fiction, particularly in its representation of the evolving character, provides the opportunity to study the motives and methods of suicides that is lacking to science (unless, of course, an individual has been under constant scrutiny and analysis for a long period before the act). And in the nineteenth century, there were innumerable literary reflections of an increasing tendency toward self-destruction.

From the beginning of the century, when large-scale revolutionary and Romantic movements stimulated millennial hopes, aspirations for social perfection, and liberation of the individual consciousness, the seeds for massive personal disappointment, frustration, and alienation were sown throughout Europe. And the predictable fruit was quick to appear in the form of dramatic Wertherian and Byronic suicides, as well as in the less obvious but equally suicidal

Romantic quests of Shelley and Tennyson. Indeed, a valid indication of the Victorians' preoccupation with self-destruction is the frequency with which it appears in the poetry of the laureate, Lord Tennyson, and its centrality in that most representative poem by Matthew Arnold, *Empedocles on Etna*. Debating whether "to be or not to be," their narrators usually argued for life, though more than a few chose death.

Recent criticism has illuminated Tennyson's morbid strain, which in the past was conveniently overlooked in discussions of his complacent optimism. In two long footnotes, Christopher Ricks, who considers the wish to be dead a preoccupation of some of Tennyson's finest poetry, lists titles of poems about suicide and martyrdom.[13] Somehow, though, the Victorians did not feel threatened by the narrowness of Tennyson's speaker's escape from suicide in "The Two Voices" nor by the poignant persuasiveness of Tithonus' plea for the mercy of eternity. It was—and still is—easy to overlook the darker implications of "Ulysses," "The Lotos-Eaters," and, to a lesser extent, Arnold's *Empedocles on Etna* since, in the first poem, the crafty leader masks his flight to death by urging his mariners "To strive, to seek, to find, and not to yield," while in the last poem the hero jumps into the crater *after* advising Pausanias how to live.

The Romantic cult of individualism and consciousness evolved into the alternative tradition of the fictional *Bildungsroman*, which emphasized the need for a young man's apprenticeship for life and ultimate integration in a harmonious society. Heroes in this mold were generally assured of long and relatively happy lives even through mid-Victorian times, when it became increasingly clear that "society" was an unsuitable, even threatening, goal for the individual. The later novels of Dickens, for example, pro-

vide "comic" conclusions (however darkling) for their apprentice heroes, despite the novels' often savage criticism of
social life. Irony—or worse, a suspicion of artistic insincerity—results when we realize that reconciliation with,
and placid existence in, society are either unworthy of the
Dickensian hero, who has passed all his tests, or unimagin-
able. Dickens would not permit himself to go as far as
Hardy went in *Jude the Obscure*. Hardy's fierce *anti-
Bildungsroman* exposed Victorian society's demoralizing,
dehumanizing, and destructive social codes and institutions;
because existence in such a society may be unendurably
painful for a decent man, Jude chose to repudiate it by
ending his life. In a novel that bewails man's cruelty to his
fellow man, Jude's defiant suicide asserts the primacy of the
individual while it attempts to disturb the world's false
sleep. It is Hardy's brutal sincerity in *Jude*, I suspect, that
makes Dickens seem less than wholly honest in the conclusions to his late novels.

While the Victorians were increasingly aware of suicide as
a spiritual and social threat, artists were not inclined—nor
were they permitted by publishers and readers—to treat the
subject openly. Hardy's scorn for such inhibiting conventions is well known, and he satirized the official reticence in
the concluding words of the poem describing the hypocriti-
cal Lady Vi: "'While griefs and graves and things allied / In
well-bred talk one keeps outside'" (*CP*, #775). When suicides *do* occur in the literature, they are committed by
madmen (e.g., Bradley Headstone), devils (e.g., Heathcliff), pagans (e.g., Empedocles), or martyrs (e.g., Maggie
Tulliver). In many cases the sting of the act is anaesthetized
by the authors' putting the victims outside the pale of
received morality or by insisting on their divine altruism.
Hardy too must rely on such anaesthetic conventions, but
his saints and martyrs are treated ambivalently, even iron-

ically, while his pagans, however attuned to modern conditions, are motivated by their ancient, pre-Christian values.

Hardy, of course, is not the only nineteenth-century novelist who seems preoccupied with suicide. On the Continent, where social taboos and editorial pressures were far less inhibiting to serious artists than in England, Balzac felt free to depict twenty-one suicides in his work and Dostoevsky depicted thirteen in his five great novels.[14] Though neither psychologist nor sociologist, Hardy had a profound understanding of the causes and effects of suffering, and the subjects that dominated his consciousness and his art reveal his sensitivity to the major social forces that disturbed the equilibrium of the individual and his society: the Napoleonic wars, social disturbances, the dislocation of rural workfolk, class distinctions, the quest for personal liberty, and decadent Christianity.

Through all the disconcerting events and movements of the later Victorian era, Hardy developed the paradoxical habit of proclaiming himself an evolutionary meliorist while writing what has been judged tragic and pessimistic fiction. Because most of his novels were written before Hardy developed his meliorism—because the novels are, in fact, more expressive of his darker "philosophic" attitudes—this study will say little about evolutionary meliorism. That subject, as Kipling would say, is another story; and it has been treated ably by a number of earlier critics.[15] Still, the latent meliorist in Hardy appears in his determined confrontations with the ills within society and within the individual. He felt that modern man must look honestly at his predicament, if he would improve it: "if way to the Better there be, it exacts a full look at the Worst." And in lines that serve as an *apologia* for his penetrating and inspiring tragic studies of love and death, Hardy wrote:

—Yet would men look at true things,
And unilluded view things,
And count to bear undue things,
The real might mend the seeming,
Facts better their foredeeming,
And Life its disesteeming.[16]

Hardy knew he could do nothing with the maladjusted universe, but with the remediable ills that afflict mankind he felt less helpless. Not a public reformer like Carlyle or Ruskin or Dickens, Hardy nevertheless perceived that all ameliorative efforts, including imaginative ones, must confront the social structure. In one way or another, to a lesser or greater degree, it is precisely to the social structure that Hardy's attention and criticism are directed. With the greatest Victorian novelists and with the acuteness of a social scientist, Hardy explored the changes wrought by massive social and historical forces upon man's feelings and experiences of the self.

Though he was unlikely to have statistical validation, Hardy must have sensed that social disorder was contributing to a rise in suicides. All over Europe, artists and intellectuals were thinking the same thing, even if few were speaking of it, and a comment Hardy makes about Clym Yeobright's lack of social ambition epitomizes such awareness. Clym "had reached the state in a young man's life when the grimness of the general human situation first becomes clear; and the realization of this causes ambition to halt awhile. In France it is not uncustomary to commit suicide at this state; in England we do much better, or much worse, as the case may be."[17] Seemingly random remarks throughout the novels—about Clym's face, for example, or the loss of pagan joyousness under the sway of the Pale Galilean, and the coming universal wish not to live—reveal profoundly penetrating assessments of modern man's vulnerability to self-destruction. A great novelist reads man's fate not on a chart or statistical sheet but in his face, in his heart. And while Hardy may have condescended to public squeamishness or editorial pressure in his indirectness and delicacy in representing suicides, he regularly created major figures who actually destroyed themselves.

CHAPTER THREE

"The Coming Universal Wish
Not to Live"

FROM HIS FIRST FICTION to his last, from Aeneas Manston to Jude Fawley, and in innumerable poems and short stories, even in *The Dynasts* and *The Famous Tragedy of the Queen of Cornwall*, Hardy provides an unparalleled gallery of suicides and self-destructive characters. In the six major novels alone, the central characters who destroy themselves are Farmer Boldwood, Eustacia Vye, Michael Henchard, Giles Winterborne, Tess, and Jude. Some minor figures who commit suicide are the neurotic invalid John South and the South Carolina gentleman in *The Woodlanders*, and Jude's mother and his son, Little Father Time. When we add to these all the characters who considered, threatened, or are thought to have attempted suicide (Gabriel Oak, Fanny Robin, and Bathsheba in *Far from the Madding Crowd*; Christian Cantle and Clym in *The Return of the Native*; Grace Melbury in *The Woodlanders;* and Retty Priddle and Jack Durbeyfield in *Tess*), we have an expanded sense of the pervasiveness of the death instinct and the fragility of so many lives in the world of Hardy's novels. For such figures, the occasional episodes of happiness in life's drama of pain are purchased at too high a price in suffering and loneliness.

But what are we to make of Hardy's most disturbing, even frightening prophecy in *Jude* about the "coming universal wish not to live"? Is it a reflection of momentary bitterness, Hardy's unguarded reaction to his domestic difficulties in the mid-1890s? Does it validate some critics' claims about the author's chronic morbidity? Or is it simply an unconsidered and unfortunate exaggeration? In any case, can it be so easily dismissed, as was done by the reviewer in the *Illustrated London News* (January 11, 1896) when he wrote: "We all know perfectly well that baby Schopenhauers are not coming into the world in shoals"?

Modern critics, with some noteworthy exceptions, have been less than thorough in treating the themes of suffering and suicide, so pervasive and so essential for the meaning and feeling of Hardy's major achievement in fiction. The ground was prepared for later workers when Albert Guerard made an important examination of Hardy's men, identifying "the 'modern man' who has lost his will to live." Guerard's seminal study first directed attention to the self-destructive impulse in some of Hardy's characters.[1] In a few brief but illuminating remarks on *Tess*, Evelyn Hardy identifies that "tendency towards martyrdom and self-sacrifice which Hardy has touched on in his feminine characters." Miss Hardy finds in Tess's determination to suffer and her passivity in obeying Angel's wishes "something abject, something unconsciously self-destructive."[2] J. Hillis Miller has provided the fullest treatment of "the spontaneous withdrawal from life which forms the denouement of so many of Hardy's stories." In Miller's view, many of the characters choose "the ignominy of death in failure" to complete the pattern of their existence: "At the end of their lives, even if they do not actually commit suicide, they come to a suicidal

passivity, a self-destructive will not to will." Miller seems to
distinguish Aeneas Manston in *Desperate Remedies*, who
literally kills himself, from Giles Winterborne, Henchard,
Jude, and Tess, who lapse into "a mild, resigned happiness"
which characterizes the mood in which Hardy's people go to
meet death.[3]

One may differ with Miller over both the mood in which
Hardy's characters die and the distinction he makes between Manston and the others; still, there is no question
that he takes suicide seriously and has sought to address it
critically. A far less satisfactory stance is the unwillingness of
some critics to perceive or admit that suicide is an issue; it is
almost as if they will not countenance a favorite author's
"seemings, or personal impressions" that appear so negative, so life denying. For example, the nature of Eustacia's
death (suicide or accident?) is still debated.[4] And in an essay
on the "coming universal wish not to live," the author
asserts that "Tess, Eustacia, and Jude *cannot* end their own
existences . . . that perseverance in the face of the horrors
of life is, for reasons inexplicable by them, a necessity." His
conclusions, that the characters' wish not to live involves
the choice of a catatonic state, a death-in-life, and that by
prescribing such a condition Hardy may have been "toying
with life by offering specious remedies," seem seriously to
misconstrue the novels, or at least underestimate their pro-
fundity and the attitude of their author.[5] Hardy invariably
refused "specious" forms of consolation when confronted by
human suffering; and even his most ironic or grotesque
representations cannot be construed as "toying" with life.

I suggest that any meaningful consideration of this very
complicated and emotional matter requires examination of
both the author's personal and artistic motives. Hardy's
fascination with violence and self-destruction, as well as his
willingness (even complusion) to explore artistically why and

how men punish one another and destroy themselves, lie behind his prophecy of a coming universal wish not to live. Unlike most Victorians—unlike most of us, for that matter, who would rather forget the brutality around us and ignore, even refuse to acknowledge, the brutality within us—Hardy seems driven to immerse himself in man's destructive element. It is this compulsion, I suspect, that causes many readers to react against what they consider Hardy's depressing morbidity. But his is not a sick vision. One could even argue that the suicides in Hardy's tragedies are sure signs of health, particularly in a man who was subject to debilitating and painful bladder infections and resulting bouts with depression and melancholia—emotions, that is, which make one vulnerable to self-destructive impulses. A fascinating study of suicides in literature argues that in the "symbolic representation of suicided characters, the artist is sublimating *his own* self-destructive tendencies." It is not too fanciful to suggest that, in distributing his own wish to die among his fictional characters, Hardy found an adequate way of neutralizing such a wish and liberating himself from it.[6] He did, after all, survive into his eighty-eighth year.

A closer look at Hardy's prophecy reveals that it orginated in his reaction to developments in the modern world. Surely Hardy, a countryman who was also a student in a great modern metropolis, was particularly qualified for registering the corrosive effects of modern thought on traditional values and the sharers of those values. Like his own Grace Melbury, he too "combined modern nerves with primitive feelings, and was doomed by such co-existence to be numbered among the distressed" (W, p. 309). And though Hardy welcomed many modern developments in science and religion, and for decades was hopeful of a union between the religious and rational spirits, he was disturbed, in his life and in his art—like his great Victorian predecessors—by the disruptive effects of much contemporary thought. J. S. Mill's "intellectual liberty" and Matthew Arnold's "imaginative reason," which offered Victorian rationalists hopes for resolving their spiritual crisis, were rarely realized; and Hardy's ideal of "loving-kindness" was to prove increasingly ineffective, and seemingly irrelevant, in an aggressive world held together by the cash nexus.

Thus Hardy's attention in his modern novels is usually focused on the "*painful* exigencies of modernism."[7] He saw that modern man is plunged into permanent doubt and intellectual crisis because of what Arnold called the incompatibility of "the immense system of institutions, established facts, accredited dogmas, customs, rules" with the needs of modern life.[8] Like Arnold, Tennyson, and Dickens before him, Hardy was aware that loneliness, depression, and ennui were becoming common moods and that exaggerated development of the intellect was causing the diminution or atrophy of natural appetites. Yet Tennyson could imagine his modern heroes mixing with action to ward off despair and Arnold's lovers could try to be true to one another, even when overlooking the "darkling plain," while Dickens' protagonists could regain paradise in an alternative Bleak House in the idyllic suburbs of London.

Such solutions were impossible for Hardy, who became increasingly convinced that modern man's self-destructiveness too often nullified love and deprived work and action of their nourishing worth. More profoundly than any of his Victorian predecessors, Hardy understood and dramatized the limitations of the essential Victorian values; and he faced more fully and openly than they the growing threat of self-destructiveness as man's consciousness of suffering withered his pleasure in living. As he grew in maturity of vision and artistic independence, he was inclined to show that the war between "modern" thought and traditional feelings and beliefs was frequently mortal, not only for the traditions but for the individuals who were left without emotional moorings after the clash. In his major figures, Hardy was aware of how vital energies within them are attacked and often overcome by opposed destructive forces that also are within them. In his tragic novels, we witness the inevitable victory of pain over pleasure.

Though Hardy never formulated a complete "pleasure principle," he had an artist's intuitive sense of the importance of pleasure as a prime motive in man's life. His notebook entry for mid-July 1888 records his thoughts about man's "determination to enjoy": "We see it in all nature, from the leaf on the tree to the titled lady at the ball. . . . It is achieved, of a sort, under superhuman difficulties. Like pent-up water it will find a chink of possibility somewhere. Even the most oppressed of men and animals find it, so that out of a thousand there is hardly one who has not a sun of some sort for his soul" (*L*, p. 213).

In none of his novels is Hardy so expansive and confident about "the invincible instinct towards self-delight" as in *Tess*. For while in *The Mayor of Casterbridge* Henchard wondered at his physical and emotional resilience, which long overcame his will to die, it is in Tess Durbeyfield that we witness the "irresistible, universal, automatic tendency to find sweet pleasure somewhere, which pervades all life, from the meanest to the highest" (*T*, p. 132). Tess's rally after her first encounter with Alec, and her love for and commitment to Angel, illustrate the workings of what Hardy calls the "appetite for joy," a "tremendous force which sways the helpless reed" (p. 218).

Despite the assertively optimistic tone of these comments, Hardy's impressions about the vitalizing force of pleasure need to be viewed in a wider context. After all, for most of her life Tess suffers miserably and, like so many others in the novels before and after her, she ends in an early grave. Like Freud (a decade and more after *Tess* was published), Hardy realized in his writings that the life instinct, the appetite for pleasure and joy, is opposed by inexorable, irremediable forces in nature and in the self which create physical and emotional pain. He notes, "In time one might get to regard every object, and every action, as composed, not of this or that material, this or that movement, but of the qualities pleasure and pain in varying proportions" (*L*, p. 217). And in *Tess* he speaks of the confrontation of two universal forces, "the inherent will to enjoy, and the circumstantial will against enjoyment" (*T*, p. 310). We can best understand what he means by "circumstantial" if we think of both the forces in the individual's external environment and his awareness of and response to them. The will against enjoyment, then, is not only "out there" in the world, but within the individual. Tess, for example, who is often seen as Hardy's most abused victim, is destroyed by the circumstances of her heredity, her poverty, her husband's heartlessness and Alec's ruthlessness; but the circumstances of her own sensuality, her ambivalence toward Alec, her unrealistic idolatry for Angel, and her inability to manage her guilt contribute significantly to her destruction.

That the momentum in the battle between the forces of pleasure and pain is in favor of the latter is increasingly clear from *The Return of the Native* onward. In Hardy's diagnosis of his world, the great antagonist of pleasure—in the individual and in the community—is modern thought. It is in the face of Clym Yeobright, the earliest of his "modern" heroes, that Hardy first locates the ravages of this new species of parasite. Thought is a disease of flesh, Hardy tells us, and the eventual triumph of thought can be read in the countenance marked by suffering and unrelieved pain. In

Clym's look could be seen "a natural cheerfulness striving against depression from without, and not quite succeeding." That the struggle can be fatal for the individual is more than implied by Hardy's comment about the "mutually destructive interdependence of spirit and flesh" (*RN*, p. 156). The thoughts that afflict Clym involve the "defects of natural laws, and . . . the quandary that man is in by their operation" (p. 185). In *Tess*, another kind of thought, "the decline of belief in a beneficent Power," is responsible for the "chronic melancholy which is taking hold of the civilized races" (*T*, p. 146).

Depression, chronic melancholy, the "view of life as a thing to be put up with": these are the experiences which many of Hardy's figures know too well, which poison that "zest for existence" which energized earlier civilizations and make increasingly difficult that "old-fashioned revelling in the general situation" (*RN*, p. 185). Like Freud, Hardy seems to have understood man's instinctual compulsion to return to the inorganic state. Both Tess and Henchard, for example, call for complete obliteration of their physical being.

Now there seems to be something terribly irreconcilable between this wish for obliteration and Hardy's conception of an "appetite for joy," the force which sways humanity to its purpose. While it is unclear whether Hardy fully understood the phenomenon and though he never formulated a concept of a death instinct (as Freud was later to do), Hardy repeatedly dramatized the monstrous paradox by which man's appetite for joy leads him to destroy himself. Almost intuitively, Hardy discerned how the pleasure principle (i.e., the desire to reduce tension and pain) serves man's death instinct. For Hardy's epicures of the emotions, such as Eustacia and Tess, excessively sensitive and susceptible to intense suffering, the only pleasure they can imagine, near the end of their lives, is the negative anodyne of death, and their choices move them inevitably to their graves.

This is the terrible vision of human self-destructiveness in Hardy's major novels. It is a frightening and threatening view, as disturbing as the so-called pessimism of Freud's later theories. Far more than his criticisms of marriage, education, and religion, this penetration of the suicidal potential in modern society aroused the fury of Hardy's moralistic and optimistic readers. His later fictions jangled the nerves of Victorians who were nearly exhausted after long periods of social and psychological readjustment to the "progress," industrialization, and new scientific and religious theories which seemed forever to shake the foundations of their social and religious faiths.

By their very nature, major transitional eras in history are characterized by both destructive and constructive tendencies; on the one hand, for overhauling traditional structures and, on the other, for creating new ones. But when the destructive energy is unchecked by a widely based faith in the future, which directs the constructive energies necessary for creating the new era—when there is no neutralization of the destructive forces, no program for accommodating change, not even a commonly held faith on which to found a program—the destructive forces are dominant and threaten a society's orderly evolution and operation. Hardy's chief fictional protagonists are too clearly vulnerable to the same forces that threatened the Victorians. In effect, his art held up the mirror and revealed to his readers their frequent inability to control or neutralize the disruptive forces which had been unleashed in their society. When Eustacia, Tess, and Jude, for example, after suffering the pains of social and psychological disorientation and alienation, ask whether life is worth enduring, their answer was terribly disconcerting to Hardy's contemporaries, for these characters rejected not only their own lives but the life of modern society. They shouted out in pain, as it were, disturbing many Victorians who were anxiously "whistling in the dark." The wish never to have been born and the desire to die are hardly isolated sentiments, expressed by disturbed or unrealistic individuals; rather, they echo through virtually all the novels.

In Hardy's fictions after *Far from the Madding Crowd* and *The Return of the Native,* there are no narrow escapes from suicide. If he permitted Bathsheba to turn in revulsion from the pool in which she wanted to end her misery, after learning of Troy's treachery, she is the last of his major figures to be so spared. Farmer Boldwood is prevented from shooting himself in the head (after he shot Sergeant Troy) and Eustacia Vye's death seems sufficiently ambiguous to allow generations of readers to believe she drowned by accident, but in both cases, Hardy's precise rendering of their suicidal nature warrants, even encourages, us to criticize his equivocation in the handling of their deaths. (I shall deal with both of these figures in appropriate chapters.)

Even in these early novels, then, where Hardy was quite willing to tone down his "seemings, or personal impressions," but more particularly in the later, darkest works, his "idiosyncratic mode of regard" and the conventional requirements of tragic fiction caused him to focus on that person, one in a thousand, "who has not a sun of some sort for his soul." However, as we consider the number of his suicides and the variety of ways by which they destroy themselves (for example, by addiction to drink [Henchard, Jude, even Jack Durbeyfield] or by sacrificing themselves to false idols [Eustacia, Giles, and Tess] and dehumanizing social pressures [Giles, Tess, and Jude]), we are increasingly aware that the percentages seem to grow higher and more threatening.

Egoistic Suicides

CHAPTER FOUR

Eustacia Vye: A Blaze of Love, and Extinction

THE CHARACTER OF Eustacia Vye and the nature of her death are subjects of interest to all readers of *The Return of the Native*. The traditional perception of Eustacia as a tragic heroine has been appropriately revised by critics who recognize her fundamental ambivalences and give due (one might even say long *over*due) attention to her unsympathetic, pretentious, even comical and frivolous characteristics. This revisionist approach is suggested by such titles as "The Other Eustacia" and "Eustacia Vye, Queen of Night and Courtly Pretender."[1] Directly impinging upon such studies of Eustacia's character is the related question of the precise mode of her death, as the title of B. K. Martin's fine essay asks, "Whatever Happened to Eustacia Vye?"[2]

Critics have long been divided over Eustacia's ambiguous demise and, quite legitimately, have interpreted it variously. The two main approaches may be described in relation to positions taken by characters in the novel: some critics, crediting Diggory Venn's guess that Eustacia fell into the weir, insist that she died accidentally, while others, convinced by Clym, Captain Vye, and Charley that she wanted to end her existence, assert that Eustacia chose to drown herself. Both groups of critics have incorporated their versions of her death in their overall readings, thereby extending the potential meaningfulness of *The Return*.

This is all to the good, for while a reader may prefer one among various readings, with a work as complex as *The Return* no single interpretation is fully adequate or desirable. The diversity of opinion among critics, moreover, is reflective of the nature of Hardy's artistic undertaking and his achievement. Because of Hardy's aspiration to emulate in his fiction the form of Greek tragedy, he made his heroine's catastrophe take place offstage, as it were, where no one could see exactly how she entered the weir. Furthermore, the conflicting intentions with which the novel closes (should it end with the deaths or the marriage, on a tragic or romantic note?), reminiscent of Hardy's difficulties in ending *Far from the Madding Crowd* and *The Woodlanders*, reveal the wide range of pressures which we know operated on Hardy from the earliest conception of his work.

In trying to strike a balance between his creative conscience and editorial directives, in transforming his rural melodrama of crime and passion into a classical drama of romantic love and aspiration, in refining the "dangerous" and demonic witch of his Ur-novel into the heroic Eustacia of the completed work, Hardy was beset by more impulses than could neatly be contained or accommodated in so forceful and energetic a novel.[3] That he gave into what were surely unfortunate "circumstances of serial publication," necessitating the extraneous sixth book of *The Return* and compromising its artistic integrity, Hardy admitted in his famous footnote by enjoining readers to choose the "more consistent conclusion." The open-endedness of this novel involves more than the fate of Thomasin and Diggory; and the diversity of critical opinion over *The Return* is attributable, to a great extent, to Hardy's ambiguous handling of two fundamental matters relating to plot and characterization: What happens to Eustacia at novel's end, and why?

The idea that Eustacia commits suicide seems preferable to the "accidental" thesis. From start to finish, Eustacia is self-destructive. The question surrounding her death, moreover, is an issue in a more important aesthetic consideration: the artistic integrity of Hardy's portrait of Eustacia. Contrary to recent discussions of "the other Eustacia" and her "split nature," and their implications that Hardy's artistry was uncontrolled and less than coherent, the complexities and even dualities of her observed character can be reconciled as components of a self-destructive person. Because her adoption of various roles fails to satisfy her permanently, she is seen as vacillating between imaginative projections of herself and submissiveness to external ideals she herself creates, such as her lover Wildeve and her husband Clym. As neither of these forms of idealization satisfies permanently, she despairs and ends her life. Paradoxically, the consistency and integrity of Hardy's portrait of a suicide require that we acknowledge the ultimate irreconcilability of alternative forces in Eustacia's nature.

While Hardy's interest in suicide predated the 1870s, it was in that decade that his close friend and tutor, H. M. Moule, took his own life (1873), an event that very likely influenced Hardy's portrayal of Farmer Boldwood in his next novel, *Far from the Madding Crowd* (1874).[4] And shortly before he wrote *The Return of the Native*, Hardy read with great interest "The Ethics of Suicide" in the *Saturday Review* (1876), an essay so interesting and important for him that he preserved numerous excerpts from it in his notebooks.[5] In his superb edition of Hardy's literary notebooks, Lennart A. Björk states that *The Return of the Native*, "written close to the time when the early notes were being compiled, shows much greater use of such material than any other novel" (*LN*, p. xxi). Björk's comments on the "numerous entries which reveal a general but profound ideological accord with Hardy's writings" are usually helpful for an understanding of Hardy's fiction. In particular, the notes from "The Ethics of Suicide" illuminate a central issue in the novel, namely, the opposition of pagan and Christian values.

> The article focuses on the conflicting Pagan and Christian attitudes towards suicide and on how this juxtaposition in its larger dimensions reflects contrasting views on human existence: "The philosophy of suicide . . . has especial interest for this reason among others, that few points could be named which so sharply and decisively discriminate the whole Pagan and Christian conceptions of virtue." [*LN*, p. 268][6]

It is my contention that the thematic structure of the novel, as well as the evolution of Eustacia's fundamentally pagan character, *requires* that she commit suicide.

From her initial appearance in the novel, when she is seen standing "so dead still" in her "extraordinary fixity, her conspicuous loneliness," Eustacia Vye is separated from the community and associated with isolation and death. She appears on Egdon Heath at the transitional hour between day and night when the land is in repose, "so nearly resembling the torpor of death." Hardy identifies her here, as he will throughout the novel, with pre-Christian paganism by placing Eustacia on an ancient Celtic barrow or burial ground. The ultimate fate of this latter-day pagan, an alien in a world inimical to her temperament, is foreshadowed when she is described as "a sort of last man among them, musing for a moment before dropping into eternal night with the rest of his race."[7] Even before Hardy plunged Eustacia into his novel's fatalistic sequence of conflicts and

misalliances, then, he imagined her as an embodiment of
the solitude and tragical possibilities so palpable on Egdon
Heath.

Hardy's poetic evocation of Eustacia immediately draws
our attention to her loneliness—what Durkheim would call
her lack of integration into the community. She introduces
confusion and disturbs the tranquility of the motionless
scene by moving rapidly, "as if alarmed," when newcomers
arrive. After "she uttered . . . a lengthened sighing," her
mood is described as a "desponding reverie." The combination of Eustacia's boredom and delusive dreaminess is characteristic of the egoistic suicide's apathy and depression (S,
p. 356). The only intelligible meaning the narrator perceives
is that the lonely person, hitherto the "queen of the solitude," "had no relation to the forms who had taken her
place, was sedulously avoiding these, and had come thither
for another object than theirs" (RN, pp. 41–42). We soon
discover, of course, that the narrator's impressions are accurate. The key notes which shall resonate through Eustacia's
life (her social isolation and temperamental despondency)
have been struck, and Hardy's placing her in this symbolic
setting prefigures her death.

Eustacia's social isolation is reinforced in this scene when
she builds her own bonfire, a symbol of man's Promethean
rebelliousness and, particularly, her own egoism. At first
the fire is thought to have been set by her grandfather, old
Captain Vye; in reality, the bonfire has nothing to do with
the community's traditional celebration. When it is found
that Eustacia ignited the fire, Susan Nunsuch says, "She is
very strange in her ways, living up there by herself, and
such things please her." So strange is her behavior, in fact,
that the Egdon rustics consider her to be a witch. The full
extent of Eustacia's estrangement becomes obvious if we

consider her domestic life and her relations with her environs, its community and traditions.

With Durkheim, it is axiomatic that the greater the density of the family, the greater the immunity of individuals to suicide (S, p. 14). Eustacia, because she has no siblings and because both her parents are dead when the novel begins, would ordinarily be more vulnerable to suicide than a person from a large family. Her father was a romantic wanderer, described as "a sort of Greek Ulysses" (RN, p. 227). A Corfiote bandmaster and fine musician, but with little money and thus socially objectionable, Eustacia's father assuaged his in-laws' feelings by adopting his wife's name and living permanently in England, where he thrived as the chief local musician until his wife's death; then "he left off thriving, drank, and died also" (p. 91).

The conciseness of Hardy's statement of the bandmaster's history must not obscure the nature and the influence of Eustacia's father's death, for he was the chief contributor to both his child's education and her romantic paganism. The bandmaster's precipitous professional failure, drinking, and death, immediately after his wife's, suggest the anomie of the widower, a condition of conjugal deregulation that frequently results in the suicide of young men.[8] Such a demise is not improbable if we examine other circumstances in the life of this wanderer, forced to work assiduously in a foreign land. The nearly complete deregulation of his existence at the time of his marriage, symbolized by his changing his social connections, his native land, and his name, does not threaten him while his wife lives and marriage provides social mooring and integration in his life. But her death, after which deregulation of the bandmaster's social circumstances is virtually complete, causes him to drink himself to death. The example of her chief teacher is not lost on Eustacia. Her own death very nearly imitates that of her father, with both pagan romantics choosing to end their lives after the experience of what suicidologists call "conjugal anomie."[9]

Abandoned at the death of both her parents, Eustacia goes to live on Egdon Heath in her grandfather's house, "the loneliest of lonely houses on these thinly populated slopes" (p. 95). Brief glimpses of their life together tell us much about the inefficacy of her "family" (such as it is) as a regulating influence upon Eustacia. In her restless wandering at all hours of the day and night on Egdon Heath and her wasteful burning of thorn roots for her bewitching bonfire, Eustacia proves "at once that she was absolute queen here" (p. 82). Later, Captain Vye comments on the romantic nonsense in Eustacia's head (p. 129). His disgust at her inheritance of her father's romanticism and his inability to govern it reveal how appropriate is Hardy's designation of Eustacia as queen in the captain's house. Still, she is an alien queen, without a court, trapped in an uncongenial land. Characteristically, her heroes are William the Conqueror and Napoleon, the continental scourges of the English.

Not only is Eustacia without a family, she is also without friends on Egdon. Her egoism separates her from her rustic neighbors, whom she calls "a parcel of cottagers" (p. 113), and she tells Clym that "I have not much love for my fellow-creatures. Sometimes I quite hate them" (p. 203). But Eustacia has not much love for *any*one. Her original lover, Damon Wildeve, she believes to be unworthy of her; she only endures him for want of a better object, and her passion for him is kindled only when he seems desirable to another. Hardy's narrator's explanation of her volatile feelings for Wildeve exposes the contortions of her egoistic passion: "The man who had begun by being merely her amusement, and would never have been more than her hobby but for his skill in deserting her at the right moments, was now again her desire. Cessation in love-making had revivified her love" (p. 110).

Eustacia will later indulge what is called her "fantastic passion" by falling "half in love with a vision" of Clym. Hardy's phrasing here recalls the mood of "desponding reverie" which took Eustacia to Rainbarrow for her dalliance with Wildeve; like him, Clym is valued only for what he might do for her. With Hardy's characteristic literalism, his narrator says: "She had come out to see a man who might possibly have the power to deliver her soul from a most deadly oppression" (p. 155). That a young woman should fall in love with a dream is hardly unusual, particularly in a Hardy novel; what is striking about Eustacia's lonesome reveries is their desperation.

It is not with men alone that Eustacia's egoism surfaces. Because of sexual jealousy, Eustacia ignored and antagonized Thomasin, a young woman who might normally have become her friend and confidante. Her "strange ways" (a quaint euphemism for her affair with Wildeve) cause Susan Nunsuch and other women—though not the staunch Grandfer Cantle—to avoid her as a witch. Mrs. Yeobright speaks for most of her neighbors when she tries to discourage Clym's interest in Eustacia: "Miss Vye is to my mind too idle to be charming. I have never heard that she is of any use to herself or to other people. Good girls don't get treated as witches even on Egdon" (p. 196). Being of use to other people has no value whatever to Eustacia, whose quest for sexual sensation leads her into "actions of reckless unconventionality."

After her marriage Eustacia, in a characteristic fit of wounded pride, deprives herself of family society when she alienates her mother-in-law by claiming, "It was a condescension in me to be Clym's wife" (p. 255). The resulting split with Mrs. Yeobright leads to a split with Clym, and believing herself the loser in her struggle with her mother-in-law over the soul of her husband, Eustacia is driven to the brink of despair. In another outburst of wrongheaded self-pity at the breakup of her marriage, Eustacia cries, "All persons of refinement have been scared away from me since I sank into the mire of marriage" (p. 334). She refers, of course, to Wildeve, her newly rich ex-lover, the only companion on Egdon she has cultivated. Mrs. Yeobright proves a prophet when she warns Eustacia against showing the fiery temper she possesses. "You, Eustacia, stand on the edge of a precipice without knowing it." When the excited mother withdraws, "Eustacia, panting, stood looking into the pool" (p. 256). These passionate scenes, so vividly and poetically rendered, dramatize Eustacia's isolation and vulnerability to self-destructive impulses. Moreover, the scene by the pool foreshadows her death by drowning in the weir. In her emotional turmoil, Eustacia, it seems, is seeking the answer to her fate by peering intently into the water.

Even when Eustacia participates in social or communal activities, her participation is essentially selfish and anti-social. Her wasteful and separate bonfire on November 5 is a form of witchlike philandering with Thomasin's betrothed lover—and not a celebration of the Gunpowder Plot. Later, after her difficulties with Clym begin and their marriage is dissolving, she attempts to shake off the gloom of her wasted life by participating in the village "gypsying," a pagan revelry that revived in the hearts of all participants the pride of life and self-adoration. When she is joined by Wildeve, she pulls down her veil and abandons herself to the dancing. "The dance had come like an irresistible attack upon whatever sense of social order there was in their minds, to drive them back into old paths which were now doubly irregular" (p. 272). Eustacia's passionate dance with

Wildeve has been called a sublimation of her sexual desire and a ritual embracing of oblivion and death, a manifestation of her "Dionysian self-destructiveness."[10]

What galls Eustacia most, and heightens her sense of isolation, is her enforced existence on Egdon Heath. Brought there from her native Budmouth, a fashionable seaside resort, Eustacia "hated the change; she felt like one banished; but here she was forced to abide" (p. 91). Her egoistic, self-destructive heart is revealed when she tells Diggory Venn, who offers her a chance to return to Budmouth, that she'd "give the wrinkled half of [her] life" if she could live in a gay town, as a lady should, "and go my own ways, and do my own things" (p. 109). But her ironical choice is to marry a man whose love for the heath is as powerful as her hatred of it, a man who would rather live on Egdon than in Paris—or anywhere else in the world (p. 220).

Frustrated in her hope of removing to Paris or returning to Budmouth, unable to overcome her sense of imprisonment, and unwilling to learn the meanings of the heath, Eustacia becomes increasingly rebellious and saturnine. A jail and a cruel taskmaster, Egdon is continually foreboding to Eustacia. "O deliver my heart from this fearful gloom and loneliness: send me great love from somewhere, else I shall die" (p. 92). The childishness of her complaint should not obscure its seriousness; it is a consistent indicator of Eustacia's character, as well as a typical warning by a potential suicide. Later, reiterating her hatred of the heath to Wildeve, she says, "'Tis my cross, my shame, and will be my death!" (p. 107). In both utterances Eustacia foreshadows her death on Egdon; but in the first, she considers death an alternative to a lonely and loveless endurance on the heath.

Eustacia's social isolation and removal to Egdon Heath exaggerate her nonconformity and intensify her gloomy depression. Without the bracing regulation of family life and familiar society—ungoverned by her grandfather, living too far from the world to feel the impact of public opinion, and scorning her new neighbors' values—Eustacia is thrown more upon herself and conducts herself solely in terms of personal interests and feelings. Her deregulation is apparent in her choosing to work when others rest on the "untimely" Sabbath. To be free of the sense of doing her duty, she would read the Bible on weekdays and sing psalms on Saturday nights; her Sunday "ritual" consisted of heavy housework and the humming of Saturday-night ballads. The narrator comments: "As far as social ethics were concerned, Eustacia approached the savage state, though in emotion she was all the while an epicure" (p. 116). Her isolation, egoism, and the deregulation of her social life cause Eustacia to suffer "much from depression of spirits." Her rebellious emotions cannot smolder interminably; eventually they must consume her.

To overcome her loneliness, Eustacia yields to what has been called the "mendacity of the imagination."[11] Having arrived at that stage of enlightenment which feels that nothing is worthwhile, she fills the "spare hours of her existence by idealizing Wildeve for want of a better object" (p. 94). In her effort at creating an ideal reality to supply the world's deficiency, Eustacia reveals her single, overriding desire in life: to be loved to madness. "Love was to her the one cordial which could drive away the eating loneliness of her days. And she seemed to long for the abstraction called passionate love more than for any particular lover" (p. 92).

The narrator's metaphors suggest Eustacia's vulnerability to a consuming emotional illness. The other key terms are her "loneliness" and her desire for the "abstraction called passionate love"; together, they breed actions of reckless unconventionality, "framed to snatch a year's, a week's, even

an hour's passion from anywhere while it could be won."
This idealizing instinct—what Durkheim calls "the disease
of the infinite"—dominates and finally determines Eustacia's fate in the novel. Throughout, she feels that want of
an object to live for is all that bothers her, and as loneliness
deepens her desire, she attempts to supply this want, first
by idealizing Wildeve, then Clym. In his diction, Hardy
emphasizes the depersonalizing and dehumanizing qualities
of Eustacia's egoism: Wildeve is *idealized*, Clym is an *object*
and a *vision*, passion is diminished into an *abstraction*. "A
blaze of love, and extinction, was better than a lantern
glimmer of the same which should last long years" (p. 92).
Eustacia shares such longings with other heroines in the
Liebestod tradition, and this passionate intensity compels
Hardy's narrator to associate Eustacia with both Cleopatra
and Heloise.

As her prospects contract and her hopes for a satisfactory
passion fail, Eustacia supplants the abstraction of love with
the abstraction of personal liberty, then with Paris and
Budmouth. Regardless of the descending order of her
ideals, the basic alternatives are always the same: a blaze of
love, liberty to do her own will, and Paris—or extinction. In
all particulars of Eustacia's idealizing, her immoderate,
overnourished imagination exposes her as an egoist lost in
the infinity of dreams. Her overexcited emotion, seizing
passion whenever possible and freed of all restraint, reveals
her affliction by the infinity of desires.[12]

Eustacia's daily existence, then, defines a pattern which
is regularly repeated: long periods of melancholy and rebelliousness, caused by her loneliness, and short bursts of
passionate and imaginative idealizing in efforts to dispel her
gloom. The price she is willing, and will be required, to pay
is apparent when she contrives to meet Clym for the first
time. After bargaining with Charley so she can take his

place in the mumming, Eustacia rouses herself to the adventure by acknowledging, "Ah . . . want of an object to live for—that's all is the matter with me" (p. 145). Like Emma Woodhouse, who falls in love with the *idea* of Frank Churchill before she even sees him, Eustacia is ready to love Clym before she meets him.

Leonard Deen brilliantly analyzes Eustacia's insinuating herself into the Christmas mumming as an action which reveals her self-destructiveness. Unconventional and antisocial implications aside, Eustacia's becoming a mummer involves her assumption of "the heroic masculine role to which she is always aspiring. She wants to alter her essential human condition, to change her sex. A dissatisfaction so thorough-going amounts to a denial of life itself."[13]

Deen's analysis represents Eustacia's motivation more accurately than at first appears. She participates in the mumming "because she was in desperate need of loving somebody after wearying of Wildeve." The word "desperate" is not to be taken lightly, for in the succeeding sentence Hardy's allusion underscores his awareness that a morbid imagination can sometimes lead directly to death:

> Believing that she must love him in spite of herself, she had been influenced after the fashion of the second Lord Lyttleton and other persons, who have dreamed that they were to die on a certain day and by stress of a morbid imagination have actually brought about that event. Once let a maiden admit the possibility of her being striken with love for someone at a certain hour and place and the thing is as good as done. [p. 160]

Hardy's association of Eustacia with Lord Lyttleton suggests similarities beyond her desperate determination to be loved by Clym: just as the lord effected his death by dreaming that he would die at a certain time, Eustacia effects hers by insisting on a life involving a blaze of love and then extinction, a life in union with Clym or death, and a life away from Egdon or death on the heath. Her self-destructiveness manifests itself in her positing of polar, even irreconcilable, alternatives for herself. Hardy seems to have understood well this form of imaginative inducement of death, which he shall dramatize most inexorably in old John South in *The Woodlanders*.[14]

In one of the strangest scenes Hardy ever fashioned for bringing two lovers together, Eustacia articulates her desperation when Clym discovers her after the mumming. He asks why she joined. "To get excitement and shake off depression," is her response. To his question, "What depressed you?" she answers simply, "Life." Some readers may find in her brief response a pretentious young woman's efforts to impress the worldly diamond salesman. But her answer may also reveal the completeness of her alienation: she is alone, with a sense of entrapment, on hostile Egdon Heath—without hope for future satisfactions, an egoistic victim of melancholic depression (S, p. 283).

Moments later, however, when they part, the pathetic self-delusion that will eventually permit Eustacia to marry Clym has begun to victimize her. Hardy describes Eustacia as caught in the *"unreasonable nimbus of romance* with which she had *encircled* that man" (pp. 162–63). The distance in Hardy's sympathetic engagement with Eustacia is measured by the words I have italicized. His metaphor of entrapment, in contrast to the figure of Tess as a trapped innocent animal, victimized by some Other, attributes to Eustacia a large measure of responsibility for her own misfortune.

Eustacia's appearance at the mumming follows immediately after an extravagant dream, a fascinatingly modern evocation of her passionate idealizing and self-destructiveness. The dream itself should be given with some fullness.

She was dancing to wondrous music, and her partner was the man in silver armour who had accompanied her through the previous fantastic changes, the visor of his helmet being closed. The mazes of the dance were ecstatic. Soft whispering came into her ear from under the radiant helmet, and she felt like a woman in Paradise. Suddenly these two wheeled out from the mass of dancers, dived into one of the pools of the heath, and came out somewhere beneath into an iridescent hollow, arched with rainbows. "It must be here," said the voice by her side, and blushingly looking up she saw him removing his casque to kiss her. At that moment there was a cracking noise, and his figure fell into fragments like a pack of cards. [p. 137]

The imagery of the dream reflects Eustacia's idealization of her lover and the life he will take her to when he rescues her from the heath. Though she believes the lover must be Clym, she has never seen him, and her dream, of course, cannot reveal his face. Ironically, the imagery of the dream foreshadows both Eustacia's paganistic reveling with Wildeve and their deaths in the weir, and it implies that this unsatisfactory lover is as close to Eustacia's ideal as she will attain. More significantly, the dive into the pool to escape the heat and attain ideal existence anticipates Eustacia's suicide and suggests this passionate pagan's motive: escape from oppressive existence into the liberty of an ideal realm beyond death.[15]

The pattern of Eustacia's existence continues after she becomes acquainted with and fascinates Clym. Her total devotion to the idealized Clym effected in her an ironic "transfiguration," which allowed her generously to yield Wildeve to Thomasin. In the famous love scene during the moon's eclipse, Eustacia manifests her devotion to Clym, her sense of time and the mutability of youth and love, and her desperate self-pity for being a lover. When Eustacia asks if it had seemed long since Clym last saw her, he answers it has been sad. "And not long? That's because you occupy yourself, and so blind yourself to my absence. To me, who can do nothing, it has been like living under stagnant water" (p. 211).

Her use of that final comparison should convey an abundance of meanings to those who are sensitive to the imagistic rhetoric in this novel. As the eclipse continues and their talk turns to the mutability of love, Clym comments that Eustacia's eyes seem heavy and she responds: "No, it is my general way of looking. I think it arises from my feeling sometimes an agonizing pity for myself that I ever was born" (p. 212). To cure her anxiety, Clym proposes marriage, whereupon she changes the subject. "At present, speak of Paris to me. Is there any place like it on Earth?" After an exercise in fatefully risky logic, Eustacia accepts the proposal but refuses to consider the future. "Only I dread to think of anything beyond the present. What is, we know. We are together now, and it is unknown how long we shall be so: the unknown always fills my mind with terrible possibilities." As the eclipse hastens to completion, she recalls a passionate love she felt for a total stranger, and the death of her love. At the end of the eclipse, when she considers how terrible it would be when she could not love Clym, he says, "When we see such a time at hand we will say, 'I have outlived my faith and purpose,' and die" (p. 215). Though the words are Clym's, their spirit is distilled from the mood created by Eustacia's romantic paganism; indirectly, they suggest her psychological orientation while foreshadowing her eventual motive for suicide.

Eustacia's refusal to end their present relationship and set a date for their wedding is phrased in terms that give precise expression to her intuitive awareness of the dangers of anomie. Secure in the present and unwilling to risk the unknown in the future, Eustacia wishes to avoid any change in her situation, even one that promises fuller happiness. "I have heard of people, who, upon coming suddenly into happiness, have died from anxiety lest they should not live to enjoy it. I felt myself in that whimsical state of uneasiness lately; but I shall be spared it now" (p. 221). That the two should actually unite, after an experience so suggestive of the evanescence of love and the terrors of time, is the final irony of this scene.

The pivotal event in Eustacia's life, of course, is her marriage to Clym. Through her marriage and subsequent integration into family society, there is the possibility that she could forestall the suicidal tendencies generated by her egoism and anomic confinement on Egdon. As Durkheim informs us, "Egoistic suicide can be reduced by reintegrating the individual into group-life, giving him strong allegiance through a strengthened collective conscience" (S, p. 17). In providing greater freedom and equality for women, the institution of marriage, seen in the long perspective of the development of civilization, has served to reduce women's anomie. What actually occurs, is that Eustacia's marriage to Clym intensifies her suicidal urge by thwarting her egoistic idealizing and by generating another severe form of deregulation, conjugal anomie.

The continuous intimacy of married life exposes every spouse's ordinary, un-ideal self. Inevitably, given Eustacia's sense of the worthlessness of the real in life, their love begins to cool, as Clym devotes himself to his self-defeating Arnoldian educational projects and resists Eustacia's pleading to relocate in Paris. Less than two months after their marriage, with Clym nearly sightless and reduced to common laboring on the heath, Eustacia is so bitter and depressed that she considers both their lives wasted. Thus marriage, which offered the possibility of reducing her self-destructiveness, becomes a "mire" and her "doom." Ironically, marriage produces the events and relationships that ultimately motivate Eustacia to kill herself.

In the chapter titled "She Goes Out to Battle against Depression," Eustacia has an apathetic, forlorn look which would have excited pity in anyone who had known her during the full flush of her love for Clym (*RN*, p. 266). So powerful is her sense of her blighted existence, she fears she is going mad. A pagan queen, living at a time when "a long line of disillusive centuries has permanently displaced the Hellenic idea of life" (p. 185), married to a man who personifies a different and apparently incompatible view of life, and "eternally unreconciled" to her life on Egdon, Eustacia first begins, seriously and consciously, to contemplate suicide. "To Eustacia the situation seemed such a mockery of her hopes that death appeared the only door of relief if the satire of Heaven should go much further" (p. 267).

She first experiences despair when she hears Clym singing while performing his menial work in the fields (p. 263). In the passionate scene when she separates from her husband, she twice expresses a desire to be killed. As Clym commands her to confess the particulars of his mother's death, she asserts, "I almost wish you would kill me." When he presses her further, she insists, "Never! I'll hold my tongue like the very death that I don't mind meeting" (p. 331). Before she leaves, she scores Clym, unfairly, for driving away her refined companions and keeping her like the wife of a hind in a hut on Egdon. "But the place will serve as well as any other—as somewhere to pass from—into my grave" (p. 334).

Having long been weary of life, Eustacia desires to end it when her marriage collapses, and she doesn't have to wait before the means of self-destruction present themselves. Directly after their parting, Eustacia wanders to her home, where she peeks into her grandfather's room; her eyes come to rest on a brace of pistols, and she regards them "as if they were the page of a book in which she read a new and a strange matter" (p. 338). It is as though the pistols convince Eustacia of the "logic of suicide"; henceforth, any arguments against it will seem absurd. Eustacia has entered the closed world of the suicide.[16]

> "If I could only do it!" she said. "It would be doing much good to myself and all connected with me, and no harm to a single one."
> The idea seemed to gather force within her, and she remained in a fixed attitude nearly ten minutes, when a certain finality was expressed in her gaze, and no longer the blankness of indecision. [p. 339]

The clause, "a certain finality was expressed in her gaze," embodies Eustacia's commitment to suicide. The wildness of her manner had arrested the attention of Charley, the half-forgotten young servant who idolizes Eustacia, and knowing instinctively that something is wrong, Charley is filled with horror at her helpless, despairing demeanor. With grave misgiving, Charley watches for any opportunity to serve and protect his mistress. His offer of an arm for Eustacia to lean on, his preparation of food and drink, and his lighting of a fire to warm her are symbolic gestures, intended to vitalize one who is inclining toward death. Accurately reading "the meaning in [Eustacia's] look" at her grandfather's pistols, and caring too much for her to let her have them, Charley removes the guns before Eustacia can use them. His solicitous efforts touch her to the quick, temporarily softening her stony immobility and dispelling her despair, but removing the pistols merely postpones Eustacia's suicide: she must await or seek another opportunity. From this point onward, she never departs from the closed world of the suicide, never disavows her suicidal vocation, never alters the logic to justify her attempt: "'Why should I not die if I wish?' she said tremulously. 'I have made a bad bargain with life, and I am weary of it—weary. And now you have hindered my escape. O, why did you, Charley! What makes death painful except the thought of others' grief?—and that is absent in my case, for not a sigh would follow me!'" (pp. 339–40).

Eustacia succeeds in ending her life on the terrible night of her flight with Wildeve, and her mental condition is perfectly accordant with the chaos of the world without. Like Henchard and Jude at the end of their lives, Eustacia finds herself isolated from all humanity; extreme unhappiness weighs heavily upon the pagan heroine as she considers whether she is to remain a captive of fate. She desires more than just "to efface herself from the country"; and, as she retains her pride, she is unwilling to incur the humiliation of accepting Wildeve as her lover. "The wings of her soul were broken by the cruel obstructiveness of all about her." Her final pathetic words reflect the childishness of presuicidal outbursts.[17]

> "Can I go, can I go?" she moaned. "He's not *great* enough for me to give myself to—he does not suffice for my desire! . . . If he had been a Saul or a Buonaparte—ah![18] But to break my marriage vow for him—it is too poor a luxury! . . . And I have no money to go alone! And if I could, what comfort to me? I must drag on next year, as I have dragged on this year, and the year after that as before. How I have tried and tried to be a splendid woman, and how destiny has been against me! . . . I do not deserve my life!" she cried in a frenzy of bitter revolt. "O, the cruelty of putting me into this ill-conceived world! I was capable of much; but I have been injured and blighted and crushed by things beyond my control! O, how hard it is of Heaven to devise such tortures for me, who have done no harm to Heaven at all!" [p. 357]

Eustacia departs from life for lack of anyone to love, of any reason to live, and to relieve herself of a comfortless existence. Hardy characterizes her soul as plunged "in an abyss of desolation seldom plumbed by one so young." She turns to the weir in revolt against her destiny and to conclude what seems to her an unjustly blighted existence. Not one of her words gives the slightest indication that her suicidal vocation has been set aside; on the contrary, the emotions she expresses are perfectly consistent with her suicidal logic.

We assume that once Eustacia is convinced of the reasonableness of ending her life, she moves directly to the weir. Her suicide is, after all, what she has chosen. However impulsive her action, however confused her motives, at the moment when Eustacia makes her final resolution to die, she achieves a kind of clarity. Suicide, then, may be a declaration of bankruptcy that passes judgment on a life as a long history of failures. In her final burst of Promethean defiance, Eustacia experiences liberation from the cruelties of Heaven: the freedom to die in her own way and in her own time has been salvaged; she fulfills her last ambition— to die. This intention, previously foiled by the watchful Charley, is unimpeded on this horrific night of wind and rain. The whole force of Hardy's artistry in characterizing her has inexorably propelled Eustacia toward suicide.[19]

When Eustacia drowns in the weir on Egdon, her death comes in fulfillment of her prophecy, her dream, and her subconscious wish. In this elemental novel, it seems fitting that Eustacia, represented throughout by fire symbolism, should die by immersion in water. The scene in which she and Clym first meet after the mumming, when he offers her water from Blooms-End, can be seen as a prefigurative or proleptic image (pp. 200–201), suggesting the direction that the timeworn drama therein begun (see the chapter's title) will take.

In an interesting and important article, Ken Zellefrow explains how Eustacia intentionally sought to reach the weir. That she drowns without struggling, without shouting for aid from those she knew were near, bears out the contention that she *chose* to end her life.[20] In fact, Eustacia is apotheosized in death, attaining therein the goal of her romantic quest for the permanence of extinction.

> The expression of her finely carved mouth was pleasant, as if a sense of dignity had just compelled her to leave off speaking. Eternal rigidity had seized upon it in a momentary transition between fervour and resignation. . . . The stateliness of look which had been almost too marked for a dweller in a country domicile had at last found an artistically happy background. [pp. 376–77]

The Paterian flourish and the classical serenity of this final view of Eustacia recall entries from the "Ethics of Suicide" essay (*LN*, p. 49) in which Seneca's advocacy of suicide as a "refuge to the oppressed & suffering" follows Marcus Aurelius' idea that it may be man's duty to commit suicide as a "means of escaping moral deterioration." Eustacia's "stateliness of look" may be Hardy's suggestion that this latter-day pagan queen has ended her life according to the "great Stoic pattern of virtue," which arose "out of a deification of human pride, which shrank from humiliation, cherished no sense of sin, & acknowledged no duty of obedience to a superior will."

My association of Eustacia's death and Stoicism can perhaps be supported by examining an earlier scene: the terrible and passionate moment when Eustacia is mortified by Clym's confronting her with her refusal to admit his mother into their home. Before Clym begins his accusations, Eustacia sees his ashy, haggard face; her guilt rendered her motionless and deathlike pallor suffused her face. At the point where the "blanching process" whitens her face and lips, Hardy's manuscript, the serial version, and the first edition of *The Return* all contain a reference that has been expunged from every edition of the novel subsequent to the Uniform Edition of 1895: "One familiar with the Stoic philosophy would have fancied that he saw the delicate tissue of her soul, extricating itself from her body and leaving it a simple heap of cold clay."[21] That Eustacia should die as a pagan, having lived her whole life as one, seems philosophically consistent as well as artistically satisfying.

Immediately before Eustacia is pulled from the weir, both her grandfather and Clym expressed anxiety over her vulnerability to suicide. Captain Vye, recounting to Clym Eustacia's recent dwelling upon suicidal thoughts, warns that "people who think of that sort of thing once think of it again." And though he is sure she would not use the pistols, he acknowledges that "there are more ways of letting out life than through a bullet-hole" (*RN*, p. 363). Later, when Clym hears a body fall into the stream, he assumes it must be Eustacia, because "last week she would have put an end to her life if she had been able" (p. 371). And after Clym accuses himself of being Eustacia's murderer he says, "It is I who ought to have drowned myself" (p. 377). These comments by the characters closest to Eustacia, coming as the novel's final words on her death, provide the finishing touches to Hardy's portrait of Eustacia Vye as a suicide.

CHAPTER FIVE

Michael Henchard:
Le Misérable of Casterbridge

IN *The Mayor of Casterbridge*, as later in *Tess of the D'Urbervilles* and *Jude the Obscure*, Thomas Hardy subordinated every fictional objective to the elaboration of the character of a single human being. The bustling market town's mayor, Hardy's splendid male creation, is worthy to stand beside his Tess Durbeyfield and Eustacia Vye. With his audacious sale of his wife, Michael Henchard seizes command of the novel in the opening chapter at the furmity tent, and with his virility, aggressive energy, and ambivalent passions dominates the book until he dies under Abel Whittle's poignant but ineffectual care. The other chief characters in *The Mayor* find their purpose and meaning in their relationships to Henchard, and the fiction takes its structure from this series of relationships, all of which involve a similar pattern: in pursuing a personal end, Henchard violates the code of social responsibility—for which he blames someone else initially, although, sooner or later, he realizes his own culpability. Though he often tries to conceal or repress his guilt, Henchard is pursued, as if by a Nemesis, and invariably is confronted by his past errors, which refuse to remain buried. When exposed, he acknowledges his culpability and attempts to repair his wrongs by imposing upon himself penalties which demean or inordinately and needlessly punish, without effecting amendment of his ways. Ironically, while his reparations are never adequate for erasing his wrongs, they function to isolate him socially and hasten his spiritual decline. As this pattern of violation and ineffective repentance is repeated frequently, Henchard loses his social position, his wordly possessions, the company and affection of loved ones whom his overbearing and impulsively passionate nature had driven from him, even his good name and self-respect (the latter are the irreplaceable credits forfeited by his intemperate outbursts). Ultimately, Henchard, the self-alienated man, is emotionally isolated and falls a defenseless prey to his characteristic melancholia. His massive, unexpiated guilt requires completion of the self-destruction on which his whole life has been spent.

The two opening chapters of *The Mayor of Casterbridge*, justly celebrated for their brilliance in launching the story of the spectacular rise and fall of Michael Henchard, present in miniature the main outlines of Henchard's character and the pattern of self-destructive behavior in all of his important relationships. The novel's opening sentence, with its casually formulaic tone, introduces us to "a young man and woman, the latter carrying a child," and locates Henchard at once within a family context. Shabby, coated with dust after a long journey, and wearing a look of "dogged and cynical indifference," Henchard seems hardly worthy of notice—unlikely ever to wear the mayor's chain. But what catches the narrator's attention, and ours, is the couple's perfect silence. Henchard's peculiar behavior, pretending to read a ballad sheet while walking, permits him to escape an intercourse that would have been irksome. His taciturnity is unbroken, and

the woman enjoyed no society whatever from his presence. Virtually she walked the highway alone, save for the child she bore.
Sometimes the man's bent elbow almost touched her shoulder, for
she kept as close to his side as was possible without actual
contact; but she seemed to have no idea of taking his arm, nor he
of offering it; and far from exhibiting surprise at his ignoring
silence she appeared to receive it as a natural thing. [*MC*, pp.
37–38]

These opening lines prepare for our understanding of
Henchard's peculiar treatment of his family, his unnatural
withholding of himself and his affections from them. The
images of separation and willed alienation from those who
are bound to and dependent upon him epitomize Henchard's egoism while they adumbrate his responsibility for his
chronic loneliness. Character is fate, the narrator of this
novel tells us, and we watch Henchard create his fate from
the very first lines in the book, establishing a pattern of
divorce and separation that will ultimately isolate him.

When Henchard gets drunk and trades his wife for a
second chance at freedom and wealth, he takes the first step
in gaining the exclusive place in the world that his ego
desires.[1] The narrator's rhetoric causes us to view Henchard's act as natural for him, though it is an unnatural violation of civilized man's deepest (if unwritten) laws, and this
startling violation of his wife and child by the drunken
young hay-trusser will hound Henchard into his unhallowed
grave. In a real sense, Henchard's drunkenness, which
nerves him to sell Susan to Newson, is both a retreat from
and a repudiation of his "better" self, the law-abiding,
generous-spirited person he can be when he is sober and
not depressed or angry. Within the divided nature of
Michael Henchard, however, the stronger force is the egoistic, anarchic, alienating self.

The second chapter begins on the morning after Susan is
sold, when Henchard returns to his senses. Hardy presents

the entire scene with masterful economy and the kind of psychological penetration for which he is too little credited. Henchard's first words convey his essential egoism: "I must get out of this as soon as I can." As he leaves the fair ground, he is relieved to escape disgrace and to go off unnoticed, and he convinces himself that he didn't reveal his name last night. His thoughts, to this point, are solely for himself: he is concerned over *his* problem and *his* reputation. When finally he thinks of Susan and decides he must try to find his family, he curses his wife and blames her for bringing him into disgrace. But Henchard is too honest to deceive himself so egregiously; and later, in a cooler moment, he realizes he must bear the shame as best he can, as it is of his own making. Before he sets out on his search, the superstitious man, in an access of fiercely self-punitive guilt, enters the sacrarium of a church and swears a greater oath than he had ever sworn before (to avoid strong liquor for twenty-one years): "And may I be strook dumb, blind, and helpless, if I break this my oath!" Henchard spends all his money in pursuing his wife for months, until he believes she has emigrated with Newson and Elizabeth-Jane. Then he heads southwestward and settles in Casterbridge, leaving the unfinished episode to work itself out to its fated conclusion.

Henchard's failure to find his wife is not simply bad luck, however; it is attributed to "a certain shyness of revealing his conduct," which rendered his pursuit ineffectual. The egoism that precipitated his action prevents him from rectifying it; and having lost his chance to retrieve his family, Henchard becomes vulnerable to "Chance" and "Change," the forces in Hardy's world that determine life when human reason and will are inactive or unavailing. Together—in this and other Hardy novels of missed chances—they conspire with a character's self-destructive impulses to assure his or her tragic fate.

Henchard's thoughts, impulses, and acts upon his awakening elaborate a pattern of behavior which is later repeated in his relations with Lucetta, Elizabeth-Jane, and Farfrae. All of Henchard's crucial relationships are with people who are actually or virtually accepted by him as members of his family. He receives Elizabeth-Jane as his child immediately and learns to love her as such—after he discovers she is Newson's. In large measure, Farfrae's immediate impact on Henchard is caused by his resemblance to the mayor's dead brother; and his company is desired, his confidence sought, just as if he *were* a younger brother (pp. 78, 115). Because of his intimacy with Lucetta in Jersey (the exact nature of which is never clearly stated), Henchard feels honor bound to legitimize the bond between them. To a degree previously unremarked in discussions that emphasize the civic or sociological aspects of this novel, the emotional force of *The Mayor* derives from its domestic character and catastrophes.

Invariably the break in a relationship occurs when Henchard, giving in to his passion, is "not in his senses." He allowed Lucetta to compromise her reputation by nursing him when he fell ill and sank into one of his gloomy fits. In a burst of jealous temper, he dismisses Farfrae, whose popularity in the town and moral ascendancy in the workyard have become increasingly irksome, and Elizabeth-Jane is treated with unnatural coldness and reserve when Henchard recovers from the shock of learning he is not her father. Hereafter, the child is left in utter solitude, since Henchard cannot endure the presence of this girl who is not his own.

Always, the "other person" is blamed for the break—at first. Lucetta's indiscretion, Farfrae's arrogation of Henchard's authority and influence, Elizabeth's scandalous language and attraction to Farfrae: all provide Henchard with temporary justification for his ill treatment of them. But his tendency to exonerate himself and conceal his errors gives way to the essentially moralistic mayor's greater need to repair his wrongs and punish himself. Nothing so graphically reveals Henchard's ambivalent nature than his "three large resolves" when, two decades after he sold his family, Elizabeth-Jane and Susan reappear: "one, to make amends to his neglected Susan; another, to provide a comfortable home for Elizabeth-Jane under his paternal eye; and a third, to castigate himself with the thorns which these restitutory acts brought in their train; among them the lowering of his dignity in public opinion by marrying so comparatively humble a woman" (p. 108). Characteristically, there is "no amatory fire or pulse of romance" in the reunion; but Henchard's determination to demean himself socially highlights the masochistic strain that, first surfacing in his swearing off of liquor, recurs throughout his life. None of his "restitutory acts" is able to erase his past or remove his guilt, nor do they effect any amendment of his ways—until, ironically, he has lost his worthiness in everyone's eyes.

This pattern of violations of human dignity leaves numerous victims in Henchard's egoistic wake. His violence encompasses his own family, as well as the high and low in Casterbridge society, but his chief victim is himself. As his actions consistently cut him off from social responsibilities and intimate relationships, Henchard is increasingly detached from the regulatory forces of social life. His isolation and his private goals and interests determine his conduct, regularly overcoming his moralistic impulses. In the absence of social control, and because of the inadequacy of the self as a sustaining goal, Henchard experiences the depression and apathy suffered by Eustacia and other egoists—emotions Durkheim attributes to their exaggerated individualism (S, p. 356).

Durkheim's understanding of the corrosive effects of social deregulation may be complemented by examining Henchard through the insights of psychology. In a highly influential study of Hardy, written in 1949 and still valuable today, Albert J. Guerard suggested that Henchard's temper and drunkenness are not the causes but the symptoms of his self-destructiveness. In portraying a character obsessed by guilt and committed to his own destruction, "Hardy recognized intuitively at least, that the guilty may also punish themselves unconsciously and cause their own 'bad luck.'" Guerard's hypothesis (which is not elaborated in his book) offers a psychological justification of Hardy's antirealistic art in *The Mayor.* Henchard's apparent victimization by coincidence and bad luck may be seen as the outcome of circumstances he has created in order to punish himself.

The mayor's relationship with Farfrae offers the best opportunity for examining the psychological processes in his self-destructive behavior, as Henchard is impressed by and grateful to Farfrae after the young man generously helps him to restore the "unprincipled corn" he has been dealing in Casterbridge. But more important than Farfrae's cooperation in an act of restitution is his appearance and demeanor, for Henchard is deeply moved by the young man's resemblance to his dead younger brother. In addition, the young Scot promises to bring modern "judgment and knowledge" to develop the business that Henchard's old-fashioned "strength and bustle" have built. He is, then, both an *alter ego,* who completes the working side of Henchard, and a brotherly companion to fulfill the mayor's need for social and emotional ties. Thus in trying to entice Farfrae to join him, Henchard offers the Scot a chance to name his own terms. Because of his loneliness and isolation from family or lovers, the impulsive mayor would have given Farfrae a third share in his business, so strongly is he drawn to him. Fraternal affection is again suggested, after Farfrae decides to join him, when Henchard offers the Scot lodging and board in his home and, later, confides in him, quite unnecessarily, about "a family matter."

Although Henchard's affection for Farfrae grows into a brotherly familiarity and, at its peak, into the deepest love he has felt for any man (p. 279), the intensity of this feeling and its implications for Henchard's character have not, to my knowledge, been adequately estimated. Farfrae is more than an employee, more than a business competitor, more than a sexual rival; and Henchard's feelings for him have the additional force of a brotherly link. However, in finding a surrogate brother—someone to abolish his gloom and loneliness—Henchard dismisses Jopp, a candidate for the position Farfrae is imposed on to take. By unfair harshness, Henchard turns Jopp into an enemy, who, like the furmity woman at Weydon-Priors, will return to hasten his downfall. More insidiously, Henchard's revelation of his secret puts him in Farfrae's power, he believes; and when they clash over Henchard's humiliation of Abel Whittle, the tyrant accuses his manager of taking advantage of him because "I've told ye the secret o' my life—fool that I was to do't" (p. 124). To the angry Henchard, obsessed by guilt and constantly beset by his shame, Farfrae's simple reply, that he had forgotten the secret, is incredible, but the mayor's guilt becomes a wedge that drives the pair apart. Henchard also turns Farfrae into an antagonist and an avenger, but, unlike his relations with Jopp, his conflict with Farfrae is complicated by his ambivalent feelings for the young Scot.

After Henchard dismisses his manager, the rift between them intensifies when Farfrae sets up his own business, so that Henchard considers the Scot an enemy and discourages a match between him and Elizabeth-Jane. In this instance, Henchard is clearly working against his own best interest, for the narrator notes that "no better *modus vivendi* could be arrived at with Farfrae than by encouraging him to become his son-in-law" (p. 136). Later, Henchard's wrongheaded resentment takes a more sinister turn when he tries to run Farfrae out of business. The narrator comments on the mayor's loss of self-control, which enabled him to become mayor and churchwarden, and his decision to engage Farfrae in a tussle at "fair buying and selling" reveals "the same unruly volcanic stuff" which prompted him to sell his wife. Nor is Henchard likely to win his economic struggle against the Scot, whose knowledge and skills are better attuned to the evolving agricultural order and whose personality and temperament are more attractive to the community of Casterbridge.

Readers of Hardy have never considered Henchard's struggle against Farfrae of the same magnitude as the sale of his wife, but if we consider the Scot, as Henchard does, a surrogate brother, the mayor's vehemence takes on the aspect of fratricide. It is not only to Abel Whittle, after all, that Henchard plays Cain. Accordingly, the severe taboo against fraternal violence creates in Henchard an overwhelming sense of guilt. As the sale of his wife precipitates Henchard's guilt, his violence against Farfrae intensifies his violence against himself. This fatal process begins when Henchard's rivalry with Farfrae takes a bitter, homicidal turn. Despite the warning of Elizabeth-Jane, Henchard engages Jopp to help him overcome Farfrae—"to starve him out."[3]

Inasmuch as Henchard considers Farfrae an *alter ego*, the self-destructive nature of his animus is obvious: attacks on the "second self" are tantamount to attacks on oneself. In nourishing murderous wishes, Henchard runs the risk of being condemned by his conscience, which demands a penalty of a corresponding magnitude. That such wishes can compel the psyche to the self-punitive act of murder has become an established truth in Western psychology, and has dwelt at the heart of Western religions and ethical systems for centuries. Psychologists call this unconscious exaction the *lex talionis*, or law of talion. Since the wish to kill is unconsciously equivalent to the act of murder, and since murder is a capital offense, the one who wishes to kill, deserves to be killed; whether there is an actual killing is more or less superfluous. This need for death is the essence of masochism,[4] and Henchard begins to fulfill his unconscious need as soon as he engages to starve Farfrae out.

The superstitious Henchard, after consulting a weather prophet, gambles on the harvest and financially overextends himself in buying up corn; however, because of his indebtedness and a loss of nerve, Henchard ignores Mr. Fall's advice and sells his stock just before the predicted change in the weather occurs.[5] Financially, he is near ruin, and when he berates Jopp, blames him for the losses, and dismisses him again, Henchard assures himself of future suffering at the twice-injured man's hands. His bad luck—as he thought it—makes the fetishistic Henchard wonder if someone might be roasting an image of him. He cannot see that his character is creating his "luck" and carrying him into ruin.

Later, when Henchard realizes that Farfrae has supplanted him in Lucetta's affection, he shows no mercy in extracting her promise to marry him. He threatens to assassinate her character if she defies him for Farfrae—though he would have pitied her had she given her heart to any other. Thereafter, his hatred of the Scot breaks out often, most notably after his selling of his wife is exposed by the furmity woman, when a moral change is discernible as Henchard descends from prosperity and honor. The sign of this change is his return to the tavern. When he resumes drinking, "he . . . committed himself to focal suicide and certain self-punishment."[6] The self-made man is intent upon self-destruction.

After twenty-one years of abstention, "the era of recklessness had begun anew" (p. 241). Just as his drinking bout at Weydon-Priors had nerved Henchard to violate his wife's human dignity, his "busting out" at the Three Mariners intensifies his violence against Farfrae. Asceticism and repressed emotionality have prepared for him a series of explosions, the first of which detonates at the inn, when he forces the choir to sing Psalm 109, directing its curses at Farfrae. Ironically, while Henchard retaliates with music against Farfrae (who had "got over" him partly by his singing), he is again vulnerable to the unconscious operation of the principle of talion, which makes Henchard himself the object of the curses he hurls at the Scot. Henchard will see the "fruit of all his toil . . . / By strangers borne away": *his* wife is plunged in grief by his abandonment, *his* seed is orphaned, and *he* shall find no one to extend mercy to his wants—except the scorned and abused Abel Whittle.

Henchard's desire to keep a choir to sing to him at the "low, dark times of my life" recalls Saul's use of the shepherd David and relates his gloominess to Saul's suicidal melancholy.[7] Since his separation from his family, Henchard has been subject to fits of loneliness as a regularly exacted tribute. The subsequent disordering of his life—Susan's death, his discovery of Elizabeth-Jane's identity, his social and economic eclipse by Farfrae, and his exposure by the furmity woman—exacerbate his anomie and nearly strip him of all that had given his existence worth and meaning. All of his losses loosen Henchard's ties to society and its regulative influences upon his life. Without a family, friend, or business, and with his drinking driving him to recklessness, Henchard finds himself alone with his painful anomie and gloomy temper, but he is not unaware of the irony of his loveless situation—the "bitter thing," as he calls it. "When I was rich I didn't need what I could have, and now I be poor I can't have what I need!"

The Casterbridge community, aware of Henchard's animosity toward Farfrae, warns the young man to be cautious.

Elizabeth-Jane is heartsick when she observes Henchard barely resist the temptation to pitch the unsuspecting Farfrae out of the granary, where the two men were working together—but Henchard is now the hired hand and Farfrae is his employer. Reflecting on what she saw (her reflections have the weight of narrative authority here), she comments on his fall in station: "His subordinate position in an establishment where he had once been master might be acting on him like an irritant poison" (p. 246). The simile makes clear the mortal danger created not only for Farfrae but also for Henchard, because of his barely constrained feelings.

Henchard's initial attempt of suicide is foreshadowed in the elaborate scene where he satisfies himself that Elizabeth-Jane is truly Newson's child. It is a brilliant piece of psychology, revealing Henchard's unconscious guilt and profound need for self-punishment. Having read Susan's letter, against her directions—and, the narrator advises us, against his own best interests—Henchard compresses his frame "as if to bear better" the scourging that had begun. Instantly, as though expecting it, he thought that "the blasting disclosure was what he had deserved." Once assured of the girl's parentage, Henchard cannot endure her sight (she too has become an avenger of his violation of Susan). His next impulse is to take revenge on his wife, but as death has deprived him of that, his passion seeks another victim. He finds himself wandering near the river, the Schwarzwasser of Casterbridge, a setting charged with images of desolation, punishment, execution. "The lugubrious harmony of the spot with his domestic situation was too perfect for him, impatient of effects, scenes, and adumbrations." In melancholic reaction to the scene and the occasion, Henchard exclaims: "Why the deuce did I come here!" It is possible that he knows—far more than he wishes to acknowledge— why he came. It will take some time, and many more visits to the bridge, before he is comfortable with the knowledge that he intends to destroy himself (pp. 145–49).

As the melancholic Samson is inexorably shorn, Henchard repeatedly gravitates toward Grey Bridge, where other desperate *misérables* had escaped from their troubles. His resolution to end his life is ordained after his final confrontation with Farfrae. When the new mayor physically removes the drunken ex-mayor from the presence of the royal visitor, Henchard, who is publicly humiliated, finally determines to even the score with Farfrae and have his postponed revenge. Though on a previous occasion he could not bring himself to tumble the Scot to his death (p. 246), this time he prepares for a mortal fight. Again he is joined in the granary by Farfrae and again they are alone, with no intruders to interfere. All conditions favor Henchard's carrying out his revenge. But his ambivalent feelings for Farfrae again prevent him from taking his life.[8]

What is Hardy telling us, indirectly, about Henchard's psychology by dramatizing his choice—on two occasions—*not* to kill the man he seems to want to kill? What kind of warrior mutilates himself, in effect, by disabling one arm before going into battle? Or is unable to dispatch his enemy when he holds his life in his hand? Or proclaims to his opponent that "no man ever loved another as I did thee at one time"? And, full of shame and self-reproach, frees his enemy to bring charges, because "I care nothing for what comes of me"? (p. 279). Such a warrior, whose violence is most effective against himself, unconsciously wishes to die.

After the struggle with Farfrae, a familiar impulse emerges. Henchard's "restless and self-accusing soul" drives him to repair the wrong he has done a man he loved as a brother, but his sense of degradation is heightened when Farfrae ignores Henchard's plea to go to the stricken Lucetta. Henchard perceives that, in his former friend's eyes, he has assumed an aspect of unscrupulous villainy. The failure of his penitential mission assails Henchard and he curses himself "like a less scrupulous Job, as a vehement man will do when he loses self-respect, the last mental prop under poverty." As he wanders near the road to Mellstock at this "time of emotional darkness," the adjoining woodland shade afforded inadequate illustration of the state of his spirit.

The contest within Henchard between Eros and Thanatos, his life and death instincts, runs rapidly in favor of death. The process of degradation that began when he broke his abstention from alcohol has gained such momentum that Henchard is shunned by all decent society and is required to lodge with the hated Jopp. Having lost all that can make life tolerable, Henchard weighs his future and sees only darkness. Like Emily Brontë's revenge-glutted Heathcliff, he has nothing to live for, although his physical vigor might keep him alive another three or four decades. "The thought of it was unendurable."

After Lucetta's death, only the kindness of Elizabeth-Jane, whom only recently he could not stand, gives him comfort and sustains his instinct to live. But when Newson appears to claim his child and take her from Henchard (as he feared), his "face and eyes seemed to die" and, impulsively, his jealous soul seizes the lie about Elizabeth's death. The desperate man believes himself subject to "visitations of the devil"—Henchard's only way of explaining his self-destructiveness. In refusing to admit the natural claim of father and daughter, Henchard makes the final error that assures his self-destruction. Though the ruse buys time, from this point on Henchard's vital instinct will diminish and offer only weak resistance to his self-destructiveness. His long journey to death seems about to terminate as he prepares to leap into the pool at Ten Hatches, but "this

unhappy man" is spared by what he considers an appalling
miracle when he sees "his actual double . . . floating as if
dead in Ten Hatches Hole." This, again, temporarily pre-
serves the superstitious man, but it cannot release him from
his suicidal vocation. Like Eustacia when Charley hid the
pistols, Henchard must find an *indirect* means of achieving
his end (pp. 299–301).

Briefly, Henchard's will to live is reasserted upon Elizabeth-Jane's removal to his house, and his return to life is
signaled by his shaving, dressing in clean linen, and comb-
ing his hair. However, Hardy's narrator describes him in a
simile, "as a man resuscitated," which implies that Henchard had all but died after his attempt at drowning himself.
Though he breathes, his wish to die makes his life a death-
in-life, and it is only *as if* he revived. The conviction that he
was in Somebody's hand begins to fade as he grows certain
that Newson will return. Then the desire to escape those
who did not want him returns, and again he wishes to hide
his head forever. We hear how little he values life, that he
wishes to wash his hands of life, that he lives against his will
(pp. 319–20). But Henchard's vacillation between life and
death is nearly over.

As Elizabeth's love is necessary for his existence, he
imagines himself as "a fangless lion," living in her home
after her marriage, even putting up with Farfrae's abuse just
to be near her. The narrator speaks accurately when he says
Henchard is "denaturalized" by his love for Elizabeth! His
decline into stealthiness and timid, agonizing concern for
her feelings suggests he is suffering a kind of chronic suicide, whereby Henchard dies slowly, inch by inch.[9]
However, when Newson returns, all thoughts of Henchard's
staying in Casterbridge are ended. He hastily packs and,
without explaining himself to Elizabeth, leaves her and the
town. Nearly a quarter century after his fatal passage at

Weydon-Priors, the ex-mayor returns to his life as a hay trusser.

In the final phase of the game between Eros and Thanatos, when Henchard hears of Elizabeth's impending marriage to Farfrae and recalls her wish to see him at her wedding, Henchard remarks precisely the effects of his egoistic nature. He realizes that his "instinct for sequestration," his "haughty sense that his presence [is] no longer desired," made him leave Casterbridge, and he decides on a last cast of the dice. Once more, he shall seek reunion and Elizabeth's love. Since he left her, she has been—as in Donne's extended conceit—the stationary leg of a compass, while he, the free-moving leg, has circled about Wessex but never moved far from her. Hardy's analogy represents the tension between Henchard's life and death instincts: "It happened that the centrifugal tendency imparted by weariness of the world was counteracted by the centripetal influence of his love for his step-daughter" (p. 319). The high stakes for which Henchard plays, and the price he is willing to pay for his gamble, are clear to him: "To make one more attempt to be near her: to go back; to see her, to plead his cause before her, to ask forgiveness for his fraud, to endeavor strenuously to hold his own in her love; it was worth the risk of repulse, ay, of life itself" (p. 321).

It is the old, impulsive Henchard who decides to attend the wedding, but the new, timid Henchard—a Samson shorn, enfeebled by solitude and sadness—lacks the force to bring off his gamble. Stunned by Elizabeth-Jane's reception, Henchard neither explains himself nor pleads for sympathy. "He did not sufficiently value himself to lessen his sufferings by strenuous appeal or elaborate argument." The circle of his life is broken; the centrifugal force is unopposed; and his last words to her are: "I'll never trouble 'ee again, Elizabeth-Jane—no, not to my dying day! Good-night. Good-bye!" After his departure, the "self-alienated man," whose nature is "to extenuate nothing, [but] live on as one of his own worst accusers," apparently "sunk into the earth" (p. 328).

Henchard never presents his wedding gift, and it is several weeks later that Elizabeth-Jane discovers the dead goldfinch. The bird, usually considered a symbol for Henchard's emotionally starved nature, also provides a means of understanding how he effects, in a month's time, destruction of a physical frame that seems fit for thirty or forty more years of life. His great size and energy have been obvious attributes of the grandly heroic Henchard; and Hardy's realization of his virility is justly admired and praised. What has not been sufficiently noticed is Hardy's skill in presenting the physical breakdown of Henchard, which begins after he bursts out anew at the Three Mariners, and its relation to his self-destructiveness. Henchard's spiritual decline is correlated with the breakdown of his massive, vital frame.

His first illness occurs directly after the catastrophic reversal of his life at the trial of the furmity woman and the failure of his corn speculation. In dazed desperation, he permits a careless business venture to debase his name, and at his bankruptcy proceeding he strips himself beyond what his creditors or the demands of honor require. When he goes to live at Jopp's cottage, he delivers himself into an enemy's hand and places himself in proximity to "the sad purlieu to which he had wandered on the night of his discovery that [Elizabeth-Jane] was not his daughter." And he is seen several times at Grey's Bridge.[10] At this point, moreover, his hatred of Farfrae intensifies as the young man gains the social and commercial status—the house, furnishings, carriage, and woman—that Henchard has recently lost. Yet his hatred is accompanied by guilt, for wanting to destroy the man he loved as a brother. It is in this context of social and psychological conditions, all working to drive Henchard to destroy himself, that his illness is to be seen.

Henchard's illness itself (which he apparently contracts by walking the meads in damp weather) is of considerable interest. As one more indication of the breakdown or destruction of a tragic figure, it possesses intrinsic dramatic importance, but of greater value, perhaps, is what it reveals about Henchard's will to live.

By a sociologist like Durkheim, the apparently senseless wandering that caused Henchard's infection would be attributed to his anomie, his exasperation at the reversal of all his habits. Such deregulation of one's life creates disturbance and agitated discontent, which ultimately seeks solace in acts of destruction against the self or others.[11] To the psychologist as well, Henchard's roaming on the meadows is far from incomprehensible. Describing the "chronic" suicide's tendency to end his life, not by a single stroke but by a series of deprivations, Wilhelm Stekel identifies a number of symptoms, including refusal to eat, lack of appetite, and deliberate exposure to chills and infections.[12] Freud also, in his study of melancholiacs, recognized that their sense of worthlessness leads to loss of the instinct to cling to life. He even posited the principle of "somatic compliance," whereby a person's unconscious impulses toward self-destruction are advanced by a kind of biological acceptance of infection, so that a person in a depressed, melancholic state may be mortally endangered by a nonmortal infection when the self-destructive tendencies are active.[13] Thus, with all the forces for destroying the self at work upon Henchard, it is not surprising that this vigorous man, though accustomed to the extremes of Wessex weather, should be laid low by a cold.

The relationship of Henchard's illness to his self-destructiveness becomes even more plausible if we consider Elizabeth-Jane's influence, for we are left in no doubt about the value of her visits to the sick man. "The effect, either of her ministrations or of her mere presence, was a rapid recovery" (p. 237). The implication is that Elizabeth-Jane's love is all the medicine that Henchard's body and spirit require, and from this time forward, the application or withdrawal of her love will affect his health and will to live.

Henchard will achieve his wish to die when his death instinct is unopposed. When he leaves Elizabeth to Newson, Henchard is an outcast and vagabond, intent to bear his punishment. He appears, however, much as he had when he first entered Casterbridge, though now his hopelessness weakens him and imparts a perceptible stoop to his frame. At the end of his day's journey, he is so distressed that he feels no want for food, and after his final rejection by Elizabeth, when he is taken in by Abel Whittle, he exhausts himself physically because of his inability to eat. Like Heathcliff in *Wuthering Heights*, after his spirit had lost its reason to continue its bodily life, Henchard perishes when his vital instincts and appetites atrophy.

His last will and testament, moreover, completes the task on which he spent his life: total annihilation of his being. In denying himself the usual rites of burial, he prescribes a funeral very much like the traditional burial of suicides: outside consecrated ground, without tolling bells, no "murners" and no "flours" (p. 331). Yet, unlike suicide notes which reveal a living man's concern with his after-death reputation or memory—those aspects of himself which "live" after he is dead—Henchard's will is devoid of such concerns, and its last petition is "that no man remember me." How vividly this illustrates the unconscious working of the *lex talionis* is apparent when we recall the final curse that Henchard hurled at Farfrae in the Three Mariners Inn: "And the next age his hated name / Shall utterly deface."

Not content with eliminating his being in time, Henchard refuses even the limited immortality that Hardy's vision affords his characters.[14] With his final will, as with so many of his previous acts and decisions, Henchard remains his own, severest judge. But, as so often throughout his life, even his last act miscarries: his immortality is assured, in part, by the pitiable but fearful vehemence of his urge toward self-extinction.

Anomic Suicides

CHAPTER SIX

Farmer Boldwood:
A Man Living outside His Defenses

F A R M E R   B O L D W O O D, in *Far from the Madding Crowd*, is the first victim in a long line of suicides in Thomas Hardy's major fiction. One of the few thoroughly interesting male figures in Hardy, Boldwood is an almost complete artistic success, and his suicidal nature is presented with the precision of a scientific case study. In every detail but one, he is a classic example of what Emile Durkheim has described as the "anomic" suicide—the one discrepancy being that Hardy, for what seem questionable artistic considerations, does not permit Boldwood to shoot himself. When Boldwood's gun is seized from him, and later, when he is granted a conventional, last-minute reprieve, the exigencies of Hardy's plot threaten the artistic coherence of a terrible and powerful character. At the end, Boldwood's postreprieve existence seems unendurable, and Hardy partially redeems his lapses in plotting when he withdraws our attention from Boldwood's life after Her Majesty spares it. Nevertheless, though in 1874 Hardy lacked the artistic authority and courage to permit Boldwood to fulfill his suicidal mission, he possessed artistic insights into the nature of the suicide in great measure. One may fairly state that of all the great Victorian novelists, none understood man's self-destructive instinct as thoroughly as Hardy; and in Farmer Boldwood, Hardy's intense awareness of human vulnerability is given a stirring embodiment.

Farmer Boldwood is a pastoral Richard Cory, a man of aristocratic dignity who seems to want for nothing in life but who, like his counterpart in Robinson's poem, is driven by his social isolation to end his life with a bullet. The "most dignified and valuable man in the parish," Boldwood is "the nearest approach to aristocracy" that the parish could boast of (*FMC*, p. 125). Nobody knew him entirely, but local gossip had it that he had been bitterly disappointed after a woman jilted him when he was young and merry. Bathsheba's maid Liddy describes him: "Never was such a hopeless man for a woman! He's been courted by sixes and sevens—all the girls, gentle and simple, for miles round, have tried him. . . . but Lord—the money might as well have been thrown out of the window" (p. 105). Rich and gentlemanly, a man whose moral and social magnitude inspires awe in the rustics, Boldwood preserved his Roman dignity in a reserve so impenetrable that he could ignore Bathsheba's beauty when every other man glanced at her in fond admiration (p. 125). So different from every other man, and seemingly untouched by common feelings, Boldwood appears "a species of Daniel" to Bathsheba, depressing her by withholding his attention.

Boldwood's distinctly outlined Roman features and his quiet, reserved demeanor mark him with dignity, but Hardy's narrator advises that Boldwood's external stillness is achieved only through massive emotional discipline. In a touching scene that recalls Gulliver's ludicrous social preferences at the end of his travels, the narrator describes Boldwood in his horse stables, pacing up and down and meditating of an evening until total darkness envelops him (p. 146). But this is too troubling to be merely ludicrous, even though Boldwood is referred to as a "celibate," visiting the place that is his "almonry" and "cloister" in one. The words *celibate, almonry,* and *cloister* suggest sublimation of Boldwood's sexual and social instincts, and this suggestion, reinforced by Boldwood's earlier association with the unicorn on Bathsheba's seal (p. 126),[1] is developed in the narrator's comments on Boldwood's extraordinary nature:

> That stillness, which struck casual observers more than anything else in his character and habit, and seemed so precisely like the rest of inanition, may have been the perfect balance of enormous antagonistic forces—positives and negatives in fine adjustment. His equilibrium disturbed, he was in extremity at once. If an emotion possessed him at all, it ruled him; a feeling not mastering him was entirely latent. [p. 147]

The description ends with a foreboding comment on Boldwood's emotional balance: "He was always hit mortally or he was missed."

On the eve of receiving Bathsheba's valentine, Boldwood appears a handsome, rich, and dignified man of forty who prefers a life of isolation and celibacy. About his past, little is known. Though it is possible "to form guesses concerning his wild capabilities from old floodmarks faintly visible, he had never been seen at the high tides which caused them" (p. 147). Boldwood's dark and silent shape is "a hotbed of tropic intensity," for the powerful forces of his mercurial temperament are contained by nearly unnatural efforts of self-denial.

The valentine and Boldwood's fate are sealed after Bathsheba, idly and unreflectingly, asks him to "Marry Me." Liddy's frolicsome prophesy that the valentine would "upset the solemnity of a parson and clerk too" is immedi-

ately fulfilled when Boldwood receives it. Continually gaz-
ing at the large red seal, like a blot of blood on the retina of
his eye, Boldwood feels "the symmetry of his existence to
be slowly getting distorted in the direction of an ideal
passion. The disturbance was as the first floating weed to
Columbus—the contemptibly little suggesting possibilities
of the infinitely great" (p. 127). These two sentences reveal
Hardy's sensitivity to the onset of anomie and its consequences in Boldwood's life.[2]

Living daily in an atmosphere akin to "a Puritan Sunday
lasting all the week," the solemn, reserved celibate seems to
have trained himself to repress his social and sexual instincts, but his stoical discipline collapses at Bathsheba's
frivolous appeal. Even before he knows its sender, Boldwood is mystified for days by the valentine, and tries to
analyze its origin and motive. A foreboding note is struck,
signifying a major alteration in Boldwood's existence, when
the solemn and reserved yeoman is transformed into a
romantic visionary. Unable to sleep because of his fascination with the letter, he tries to contend with the ubiquitous
presence of the unknown writer.

> The *vision* of the woman writing, as a supplement to the words
> written, had no individuality. She was a *misty* shape, and well
> she might be, considering that her original was at that moment
> sound asleep and oblivious of all love and letter-writing under the
> sky. Whenever Boldwood dozed she took a form, and com-
> paratively ceased to be a *vision*: when he awoke there was the
> letter justifying the *dream*. [p. 128; my italics]

There is no little pathos in the respectable farmer's impassioned visionings. Upon entering what psychiatrists today
would call a "mid-life crisis," Boldwood embodies Hardy's
lifelong ambivalence toward what his generation saw as the
imaginative excesses of Romanticism. Despite his tempera-

mental attachment to the ideals of the "visionary company" of Shelley, Keats, and Swinburne, Hardy understood the practical dangers of trying to live in terms of romantic dreams. Typically, in Hardy's fictions, a character must be prepared to deal with the crucial opportunities or threats in his or her life with judgment, or controlled reason and good sense (Gabriel Oak is the obvious example), but when one's impressions of reality are in the unreliable form of dreams or visions, as with Eustacia and Jude and Sue, there is usually trouble or pain, or both, ahead. Boldwood is in real danger henceforth, as Hardy's dreamers are rarely survivors.

The effects of Bathsheba's disruption of Boldwood's equilibrium are strikingly evident after he receives her letter. After tricking Oak into revealing Bathsheba as the sender of the valentine, Boldwood feels "twinges of shame and regret at having so far exposed his mood by those fevered questions to a stranger" (p. 139). The importance of those twinges should not be underestimated, for Boldwood is characterized in terms of his Roman dignity and stoic commitment to personal honor. Shortly afterward, just before Boldwood first approaches Bathsheba, the narrator provides a fuller analysis of the disturbance or deregulation in Boldwood's life: "A man's body is as the shell, or the tablet, of his soul, as he is reserved or ingenuous, overflowing or self-contained. There was a change in Boldwood's exterior from its former impassibleness; and his face showed that he was now living outside his defenses for the first time, and with a fearful sense of exposure" (p. 148).

Accompanying Boldwood's experience of deregulation is an affliction Durkheim calls "the disease of the infinite." This disease assumes different forms, but in the anomic suicide, when emotion is overexcited and freed from all restraint, the potential suicide loses himself in the "infinity" of his desires (S, p. 287). Boldwood's first symptoms appear in his idealization of Bathsheba, "this romance in the flesh." When he takes his first serious look at her, his mind is quickly made up and his heart begins to move within him. "To the best of his judgment neither nature nor art could improve this perfect one of an imperfect many" (*FMC*, p. 143). A man who lives outside his defenses needs better judgment than Boldwood shows—particularly when, after years of emotional restraint and celibate living, he judges a woman. His jealousy while watching Bathsheba trade corn with a young farmer is instinctual and he feels an angry impulse to thrust himself between them, an ominous foreshadowing of his later dealings with Sergeant Troy. But he renounces the idea because "it was debasing loveliness . . . and jarred with his conceptions of her" (p. 144).

Thus even before Boldwood addresses Bathsheba, he has taken the first steps on his journey toward self-destruction, and the narrator describes the fated farmer just before he speaks to Bathsheba. Without a family or other sustaining social ties, Boldwood lacks the usual insulation against the dangers of loneliness, and his vulnerability to suicide is proleptically symbolized by Hardy's placing him by a gate where he was "overhung by a willow tree in full bloom."

> The insulation of his heart by reserve during these many years, without a channel of any kind for disposable emotion, had worked its effect. It has been observed more than once that the causes of love are chiefly subjective, and Boldwood was a living testimony to the truth of the proposition. No mother existed to absorb his devotion, no sister for his tenderness, no idle ties for sense. He became surcharged with the compound, which was genuine lover's love. [p. 148]

Boldwood's first words (pp. 152–54) are pregnant with foreboding, revealing his anomie, his idealization of Bathsheba, his investment of his whole emotional being in the idea of union with her, and his sense of the pain of existence without her:

> "I feel—almost too much—to think," he said, with a solemn simplicity. "I have come to speak to you without preface. My life is not my own since I have beheld you clearly, Miss Everdene—I come to make you an offer of marriage."

> "I had never any views of myself as a husband in my earlier days, nor have I made any calculation on the subject since I have been older. But we all change, and my change, in this matter, came with seeing you. I have felt lately, more and more, that my present way of living is bad in every respect. Beyond all things, I want you as my wife."

> "My life is a burden without you," he exclaimed, in a low voice. "I want you—I want you to let me say I love you again and again!"

> "I want you for my wife—so wildly that no other feeling can abide in me; but I should not have spoken out had I not been led to hope."

> "I cannot say how far above every other idea and object on earth you seem to me—nobody knows—God only knows—how much you are to me!"

After vehement pleading for her kindness and condescension in considering whether she can bear with him as a husband, Boldwood promises to give Bathsheba time to reconsider her rejection of his proposal. Far from the distinterested proposal Bathsheba considers it, the narrator says that the "rarest offerings of the purest loves are but a self-indulgence, and no generosity at all" (p. 155).

As Boldwood's hope for union with Bathsheba waxes and wanes, his anomie intensifies as Bathsheba becomes the sole purpose of his existence. Even when his prospects seem most promising, he is moved with restlessness and with what Keats calls a "too-happy happiness." "This unwonted abstraction by love of all dignity from a man of whom it had ever seemed the chief component, was, in its distressing incongruity, a pain to [Bathsheba] which quenched much of the pleasure she derived from the proof that she was idolized" (p. 180). Like Henchard, he is "denaturalized."

Even in Bathsheba's eyes, the gentlemanly farmer is discernibly in decline. Though he had previously been associated with the eagle, symbolical of Roman grandeur (p. 127), Boldwood has taken on the "sorry look of a grand bird without the feathers that make it grand" (p. 181). It is significant that Boldwood's decline—we might even say degradation—is in large degree attributable to his self-indulgent love. Clearly, Hardy implies, the farmer is victimized from within as well as from without.

Hardy's awareness of the relationship between frustrated love and spiritual desolation is made obvious in a pivotal speech that Troy addresses to Bathsheba. After her capitulation to his flattery, in what the narrator calls a moment that was the turning point of a career, Troy continues:

> "Such women as you a hundred men always covet . . . you can only marry one of that many. Out of these say twenty will endeavour to drown the bitterness of despised love in drink; twenty more will mope away their lives without a wish or attempt to make a mark in the world, because they have no ambition apart from their attachment to you; twenty more—the susceptible person myself possibly among them—will be always draggling after you, getting where they may just see you, doing desperate things." [p. 194]

Troy's love, of course, is not despised, nor is he as susceptible as he would like Bathsheba to believe. However, his remarks foreshadow the fate that is imminently to befall Farmer Boldwood, who is truly the "susceptible person."

Bathsheba's encouragement of Boldwood is followed by rejection of his suit when she becomes fascinated by Sergeant Troy. This pattern of arousal and frustration of Boldwood's hopes is repeated later in the novel, after the rumor of Troy's drowning makes Bathsheba, his widow, available again. It is typical of Hardy's fiction that a character is put in the same situation again, or is required to make a particular choice again, and fails to act effectively or chooses wrongly both times. This technique of allowing a second chance often reveals that it is not simply fate or bad luck that victimizes Hardy's characters; rather, their failures and wrong choices demonstrate incapacity to perceive one's best interests or, where a character knows how to act but cannot choose so to act, the paradoxical inability to serve one's own needs.

In both instances when Boldwood's hope to marry Bathsheba is aroused and then frustrated, he experiences an intensification of anomie. When he met her after she first rejected him, his "manner was stunned and sluggish." The discovery that his idol is no more consistent than her fellows came as "no less a scourge than a surprise." After describing his feeling for her as "strong as death," Boldwood bursts out and begs her pity. "God's sake, yes—I am come to that low, lowest stage—to ask a woman for pity! Still, she is you—she is you" (pp. 219–20). In this painful loneliness he continues: "I am beyond myself about this, and am mad. . . . I am no stoic at all to be supplicating here; but I do supplicate to you. I wish you knew what is in me of devotion to you; but it is impossible, that. In bare human mercy to a lonely man, don't throw me off now!" This is followed by his vacillation between trying to renounce her and laboring humbly for her again. Bathsheba feels deep pity for the suffering farmer and repents of her childish games. Without knowing fully the prophetic truthfulness of her words, she says, "How was I to know that what is a pastime to all other men was death to you?" (p. 221).

Boldwood's intense ambivalence reveals itself in his illogical alternation of emotions. After begging Bathsheba's pity, he mourns the loss of his self-respect and public standing; then reviles, curses, and threatens Sergeant Troy. This wild and delusory train of emotions, ending with Boldwood's physical exhaustion after tenderly and protectively exculpating Bathsheba, provides a number of signposts that indicate the direction of Boldwood's movement. He seems for the first time to have entered the "closed world" of the suicide: experiencing the world as wholly alien, he first despairs and considers his own death. His self-pity sounds the note of childishness, a typical emotion of the potential anomic suicide.[3]

> Now the people sneer at me—the very hills and sky seem to laugh at me till I blush shamefully for my folly. I have lost my respect, my good name, my standing—lost it, never to get it again.
>
> As for me, I had better go somewhere alone, and hide—and pray. I loved a woman once. I am now ashamed. When I am dead they'll say, Miserable love-sick man that he was. Heaven-heaven—if I had got jilted secretly, and the dishonour not known, and my position kept! But no matter, it is gone, and the woman not gained. [pp. 222–23]

Boldwood's melancholy concern over his dishonor and loss of respect represents far more than wounded social pride; it reveals the depth of his fundamentally Roman commitment to personal honor—the loss of which, as Freud suggests, renders life both shameful and worthless.[4] It is Boldwood's tragic misfortune to experience the resurgence and frustration of his marital hopes at least twice again before he finally kills Troy.

On numerous occasions before the shooting, Boldwood's "suicidal vocation" is strongly indicated. After his efforts to bribe Troy into leaving Bathsheba miscarry, he realizes it would be a mistake to kill his rival, as he had threatened; then he considers it far better to kill himself (p. 247). Dogged by despair thereafter, on the night of the rainstorm that ruins him financially, Boldwood appears strangely altered to Gabriel. Oak's astonishment at Boldwood's irresponsible husbandry is a most revealing measure of Boldwood's anomie. In an effort to relieve his heart, Boldwood admits to Oak that he cannot fend off his grief, that he has lost his belief in God's mercy, and that he feels it is better to die than to live (pp. 270–71). His behavior reveals many symptoms of the melancholiac: profoundly painful dejection, abrogation of interest in the outside world, inhibition of all activity, and a lowering of self-regarding feelings that finds utterance in self-reproach and culminates in a delusional expectation of punishment.[5]

When Troy is reported drowned, Boldwood's unreasoning devotion leads him to hope again to have Bathsheba. The narrator characterizes this devotion as "a fond madness which neither time nor circumstance, evil nor good report, could weaken or destroy" (p. 339). The "disease of the infinite" has advanced to a dangerous degree. Again, fevered hopes and wildly self-indulgent dreams impel him to strike a bargain with Bathsheba for her hand, by which her promise to marry him is nearly extorted. His latent passion erupts as he coerces Bathsheba to name the day of the wedding. "You wouldn't let a dog suffer what I have suffered, could you but know it! . . . Be gracious, and give up a little to me, when I would give up my life for you!" Gaining her assent, he says: "I am happy now . . . God bless you!" (pp. 375–76). Well might Bathsheba fear that she holds the man's fate in her hands.

A crucial reversal, in the plot and for Boldwood, occurs when the long-lost Troy reappears to reclaim Bathsheba, only moments after Boldwood received her promise. The narrator portrays Troy as a persistent Satan who has come again to break in upon Boldwood's bliss, scourge him, and snatch away his delight a second time. Transformed by despair, Boldwood enters the anomic suicide's final phase,[6] when anger and disappointment unleash violence against a person to whom the suicide imputes all his unhappiness. Bathsheba's scream when Troy grips her arm still fills the air, while Boldwood, a frenzied look in his eye, discharges his gun at Troy. Like a Roman Stoic, who would secure his personal honor by liberating himself from a life of unendurable pain, Boldwood prepares to fire again; but before he can turn the second barrel on himself, Samway interferes. "'Well, it makes no difference!' Boldwood gasped. 'There is another way for me to die'" (p. 379)—whereupon he kisses Bathsheba's hand, puts on his hat, and in a steady, even pace walks directly to jail, to pay with his life for his capital offense. In his suicidal effort, he seems to retrieve the dignity he lost in pursuing Bathsheba.[7]

Thus ends Boldwood's tragic and inexorable journey toward self-destruction. His determination to end his life is fully consistent with the character he has become through his experience with Bathsheba, and fully consonant with the behavior of an anomic suicide. Typically, such an individual goes to death in anger, his death being preceded by the murder of someone he accuses of having destroyed his existence. His exasperation is most obvious when expressed in the form of homicide or some other violent outburst, whereupon, in an access of anger, the anomic suicide attacks the self.[8] Boldwood's experience, then, is a paradigm of the anomie of the unmarried man, whose desire, when it is free from the influence and normal restraints of society, lacks the ability to check itself.

Two matters require further consideration: the central questions of the farmer's moral responsibility and his motivation at the time he attempted to shoot himself. That the farmer was insane when he shot Troy is generally believed, especially after discovery of the elegant clothes and jewelry he had locked away, pending his union six years later with "Bathsheba Boldwood" (p. 385). This powerful presumption of madness is rendered credible in view of the suspected madness in his family (p. 252), Bathsheba's earlier concern over his mental instability (p. 358), and his "unprecedented neglect of his corn stacks in the previous summer" (p. 386); and this prejudice prompts Boldwood's merciful neighbors to "remove the crime, in a moral point of view, out of the category of wilful murder, and lead it to be regarded as a sheer outcome of madness" (p. 386).

But Hardy's narrator strikes a very ambiguous tone about the presumed insanity, and more importantly, Gabriel Oak, whose judgment in serious matters has served as a standard throughout the novel, tells Smallbury that he cannot honestly say he believes that Boldwood was out of his mind when he shot Troy. This judgment of Oak's, the novel's last word on the subject, strikes me as authoritative. Hardy seems to have been free of the traditional belief that suicides are either evil or mad; more importantly, the consistency of his portrait of an anomic, honorable farmer, of Roman bearing and Stoic temper, seems to demand the *responsible* choice of death.

The authenticity of Boldwood's suicide, finally, can be verified if we consider his motivation before he attempted to take his life. Freud's seminal work on melancholia, which resulted in his complicated explanation of suicide as "transposed murder," can perhaps illuminate Boldwood's motives. For Freud, the suicidal process begins with a wish to kill someone whom the suicide had loved and whose being had been introjected into the suicide's self. Because this person could not or ought not be killed, the suicide directs his aggression against the self that has been identified with the intended victim through ego splitting.[9]

The process is brilliantly dramatized in chapter 31, "Blame—Fury," where Boldwood is first "awakened to woman's privileges in tergiversation even when it involves another person's possible blight." Stunned, sluggish, Boldwood nevertheless sees that Bathsheba fears his violent nature. In alternately begging and rejecting her pity, Boldwood blames Bathsheba for drawing him to her, then turning him away. His tone becomes resentful when she rejects his final pleas for her love, and threatening when he reviles her for perfidy in turning to Troy. Boldwood's vehemence then turns away from Bathsheba and issues in violent threats against her lover; however, he seems to sense that the threats are really aimed at her, and he drops "his voice suddenly and unnaturally. 'Bathsheba, sweet, lost coquette, pardon me! I've been blaming you, threatening you, behaving like a churl to you, when he's the greatest sinner.'"

Though he can withdraw from her presence, he cannot call back his words and their revelation of his dangerous feelings toward her. And when, finally, he warns Bathsheba to keep Troy out of his presence for fear he may be tempted beyond himself, he seems aware that Bathsheba, in her complicity with Troy, might be equally vulnerable to his fury (pp. 218–24). His final "courtesy" to Bathsheba, after he kills Troy, is in sacrificing himself rather than shooting her.

Hardy's portrayal of Farmer Boldwood is a nearly complete artistic triumph. His perception of the moral and psychological consequences of Boldwood's social isolation is thorough and convincing. Only in the last-minute reprieve does Hardy's rigorous artistry flag; with this event, the manifest influence of George Eliot's *Adam Bede* seems both unfortunate and detrimental. However, Hardy's consideration of his readers' wish for a happy ending surely accounts in part for the reprieve. Also, his determination to conclude the novel on a note of reconciliation may have influenced his decision to imprison Boldwood. Certainly, his suicide would have shrouded the novel's conclusion and distracted attention from the reunion of Oak and Bathsheba. It is difficult to conceive, though, that Hardy shared Her Majesty's pleasure in remitting Boldwood's capital sentence.

Stripped of his honor and deprived of all hope for love, Boldwood is a pitiable figure. Even the Roman Stoic's privilege of self-liberation through suicide is withheld from him. Under these circumstances, the prolongation of his life seems almost inhumane—an attitude we rarely associate with the sympathetic Thomas Hardy.

CHAPTER SEVEN

Jude Fawley:
"Why Died I Not from the Womb?"

B ECAUSE OF PUBLIC EVENTS which made marriage and divorce the chief topics of discussions when *Jude the Obscure* appeared, some reviews of the novel and much subsequent scholarly comment have been preoccupied to an exaggerated degree with those issues and other "problems." There is, of course, a legitimate sense in which *Jude* can be considered Hardy's anatomy of modern civilization and its discontents, but for all its concentration upon the ills and problems of contemporary life—the need for reforms in education and in the church; the social problems of marriage, divorce, and repressive public opinion; and the spiritual problems of modern alienation and "unrest"—*Jude* is essentially the story of an obscure man's life. From the time Hardy jotted the note which was the germ for the story, through his experimentation with various titles, and for years after the book was published, his central interest had been fixed on the experience of "a young man—'who could not go to Oxford'—His struggles and ultimate failure. Suicide" (*L*, pp. 207–8). The young man's nature is suggested by the provisional titles under which the novel originally appeared: he is something of a simpleton, a dreamer, a recalcitrant, a heart insurgent; his fate is to take the fictional form of a "tragedy of unfulfilled aims" as he experiences within himself the "deadly war waged between flesh and spirit."[1]

What needs to be emphasized is that divorce, dogmatic religion, and snobbish barriers to academic training, as symbols of separation and alienation, are among the many experiences which account for Jude's isolation, depression, despair, and suicide. When the heart of this novel is distinguished from the fictional skeleton and machinery which support it, *Jude the Obscure* emerges as a personal history, a novel dominated by a character whose life reflects the spirit of the age and whose defiant death repudiates it.

Hardy's original conception of his "young man" included his "suicide," after a "deadly" war and the shattering of his ideals, and his portrait of Jude Fawley is an elaboration of that self-destructive protagonist. A remarkably "modern," even prophetic figure, Jude seems afflicted by the "disease of consciousness" and is extremely vulnerable to that abnormally developed faculty within him. Dostoevsky has written that "suffering is the sole origin of consciousness," and Jude's life gives the ring of authority to the Russian's axiom. At the age of eleven, Jude had already "felt the pricks of life somewhat before his time" (*J*, p. 35). He is first seen shedding tears at the departure of the local schoolmaster, who had been the initiator of his academic aspirations, and he is shortly fired by Farmer Troutham because of his refusal to scare away the rooks, pathetic alter egos who also live in a world which does not want them. Dostoevsky's narrator in *Notes from Underground* comments upon the kind of man Jude is fated to become: "I swear, gentlemen, that to be too conscious is an illness—a real thoroughgoing illness. For man's everyday needs, it would have been quite enough to have the ordinary human consciousness, that is, half or a quarter of the amount which falls to the lot of a cultivated man of our unhappy nineteenth century."[2]

Early on, Hardy's narrator prophesizes a painful future for the young man, who is acutely conscious of widespread suffering in the world: "This weakness of character, as it may be called, suggested that he was the sort of man who was born to ache a good deal before the fall of the curtain upon his unnecessary life should signify that all was well with him again" (*J*, p. 41).

Jude's initial experiences of separation establish the loneliness which is his definitive emotional condition. After his mother drowns herself and his father dies, Jude feels himself a "poor useless boy," alienated from the ugly and lonely landscape, and unwanted by anyone, including the aunt who had taken him in. His sense of worthlessness at being unloved is reflected in his sympathy for the puny and sorry birds whose lives resemble his own, and his exaggerated sense of guilt makes him fear he has wholly disgraced himself and become a burden to his great-aunt for life (pp. 38–42). Very early in his life, Jude experiences a fit of despondency over his existence; because he perceives horrid cruelty in nature and the uselessness of his own, undemanded existence, Jude desires to prevent himself from growing up and becoming a man. Though this desire is transient, it will be recurrent, and his denial of life will intensify as he learns more thoroughly the meaning of his life.

For the emotionally deprived youth, bereft of the supports normally provided by parents and siblings, the schoolmaster emerges as a surrogate father. Phillotson fosters the boy's fondness for books and instills in him a fascination for the university at Christminster. The local physician, Vilbert, also raises Jude's hopes for intellectual advancement, but the shoddy quack's failure to send books devastates the boy, and Jude's intense frustration at his assumed inability to learn from the books Phillotson *did* send makes him miserable. This latter experience (which Hardy's narrator satirizes gently by noting that it lasted a full quarter of an hour) reflects the author's persistently ambivalent feelings about the too-sensitive lad. Surely there is a ludicrous, overly theatrical note of adolescent abandonment here. Still, Jude is unconsoled and continues "to wish himself out of the world" when nobody comes to cheer him out of his remorse. The relationship between his loneliness, frustration, and despair is presented quite directly, and Jude's desolation is nonetheless dangerous because of Hardy's humorous exhibition of it (pp. 53–55).

Book learning is an important form of education for Jude, whose relations to the typical heroes of Victorian *Bildungsromane* are antithetical,[3] and for some years books are both a lodestar and a refuge for the lonely young man. However, the chief type of education he gains is a culture of the spirit. In D. H. Lawrence's terms, Jude learns about what "he held in his blood," and this part of his education is conducted at the hands of Arabella and Sue.[4] Jude's entrapment by Arabella, a sordid piece of low comedy, occurs because of a sexual urge to embrace a woman for whom he had no respect and whose life has virtually nothing in common with his own. Jude knows Arabella is "not worth a great deal as a specimen of womankind," but tries to convince himself that his "factitious belief in her" is what really matters (pp. 80–81). Against all reason and the urging of his will, Jude closes his New Testament and enters into the foolish covenant with a barmaid. What is crucial in the affair is his capacity for violating his own interests by opposing the impulses of his better self.

When he forgoes his academic studies to marry the deceitful Arabella, Jude seems unusually willing to martyr himself. Having grown up feeling worthless and useless,

Jude considers himself of little value as an individual. Unlike the egoist, who obeys only the self's commands, Jude's decision to marry is altruistic and, actually, opposed to the self's well-being. So powerful are the collective forces of local customs, conventional morality, and a guilty social conscience that they undermine his life's hope by compelling him to do the "honorable thing." This is the first of numerous occasions when his naive altruism proves him to be an enemy of the self. Like the shorn Samson he becomes in marriage, Jude will have to pull his life down around him to release himself from his folly.

The fiasco of Jude's and Arabella's marriage is over quickly, and their lives are ruined, he thinks, by the fundamental error of basing a permanent relationship on temporary and transient feeling. Deeply disturbed by the apparent meaninglessness of the future and struck by the congruency of his marital situation to that of his parents', Jude attempts to drown himself, as his mother had done. With this insightful scene, Hardy exhibits his understanding of the fatal power of suggestion in the suicidal acts of parents. But when Jude is unable to crack the ice on the lake and is spared a frigid death by drowning, he seeks an alternative form of self-destruction. "What might such a degraded man do who is not sufficiently dignified for suicide?" he asks himself. "He could get drunk. . . . Drinking was the regular, stereotyped resource of the despairing worthless. He began to see now why some men boozed at inns" (p. 94).

Jude's separation from Arabella, an instance of conjugal anomie, reveals how premature marriages bring about a harmful moral state, especially in men (S, p. 179). Coming on the heels of the blasting of his academic dreams, it introduces massive emotional disorder into Jude's lonely, guilty existence. His suicide attempt and drunkenness, the

immediate indications of his vulnerability to self-destruction, complete a cycle of behavior that will recur until a later
cycle ends with a "successful" attempt. From this moment,
Jude's sensitive nature will be shaken by impossible dreams
and desires, which will regularly be frustrated, and which
create an ultimately intolerable state of disturbance, emotional agitation, and discontent.

After Arabella leaves Jude, he is free to start his life anew;
but his is the freedom of anomie, in which one's desire, at
liberty to attach itself where and to whom it will, cannot
check itself—cannot become fixed when it is uncertain of
retaining what attracts it. When hope resurfaces after he
sobers up, Jude decides to recommit himself to a career at
Christminster. Though knowledge and self-development
motivate him, the decision is primarily emotional. It is
undertaken after Jude has been aroused by a photograph of
his cousin, Sue Bridehead, who is living and working in the
university town. The dreamlike unreality of Jude's attraction
to both the university and to Sue is suggested by a halo he
sees surrounding each of them (J, pp. 97, 102), and they are
to be the ruling passions of his life henceforth. Jude hopes at
Christminster to find "something to anchor on, to cling to";
and after meeting Sue, he feels he has "at last found an-
chorage for his thoughts, which promised to supply both
social and spiritual possibilities." Clearly, Sue is more necessary for Jude's social needs, for he realizes, upon entering
Christminster, the "isolation of his own personality." Using
the symbol of an anchor for both Sue and Christminster (pp.
49, 115), Jude emphasizes their potential value for securing
him from his otherwise directionless, meaningless
existence.

Almost at once, however, Jude is forced to reexamine his
dreams about Christminster. His disillusionment begins the
morning after he arrives, when he is beset by impressions of

the barbarism, rottenness, defectiveness of the place. Throughout that first day he remains in loneliness and begins to perceive how far away from the object of his enthusiasm he really was. At the end of the day, the last voice he hears from the university's venerable past lullabies him to sleep with the prophetic lines:

> Teach me to live, that I may dread
> The grave as little as my bed.
> Teach me to die.

His academic frustrations are prefigured, moreover, when he realizes that only a wall divides him from others with the same intellectual desires—"but what a wall!" (p. 109). Ironically, Jude's experiences at Christminster nevertheless teach him to live as a self-asserting individual, instead of as a worthless altruist whose life may be sacrificed to external ideals, and he will learn to die when society refuses to countenance his experiments in personal liberty, even though they harm none of its members.

When Jude realizes the hopelessness of his chances for matriculating at Christminster, given his unsystematic, untutored study and his insufficient finances, he looks back at his diligent efforts to learn Latin and Greek, his reading in the Griesbach text of the New Testament and in the Greek tragedians, and he recalls Heine: "Above the youth's inspired and flashing eyes / I see the motley mocking fool's-cap rise!"[5] Jude knows that his destiny is to be among "the manual toilers in the shabby purlieu" of Christminster, among the struggling men and women who "were the reality of Christminster."

Previously, he had a "true illumination" about the worth and dignity of his stonecutting (p. 108), and he tries to convince himself that he could renounce his scholarly ambition with a smile if he could have Sue as a companion. But when he receives Tetuphenay's "terribly sensible advice," to keep to his trade, Jude feels deprived of the objects of both intellect and emotion. His hopeless relations with Sue drive him to blaspheme in a pub, his depression leads to drunkenness, and in his shame and remorse he cries out to Sue: "I could not bear my life as it was! . . . O, do anything with me, Sue—kill me—I don't care! Only don't hate me and despise me like all the rest of the world!" (p. 143). Hardy's narrator suggests the danger to Jude's spirit when he compares the effects of this failure in love and ambition to those of Jude's separation from his wife: "He thought of that previous abyss into which he had fallen before leaving this part of the country; the deepest deep he had supposed it then; but it was not so deep as this. That had been the breaking in of the outer bulwarks of his hope: this was of his second line" (p. 145). Jude correctly diagnoses his condition when he confesses that he has become "melancholy mad, what with drinking and one thing and another."

Jude, of course, cannot have Sue at this time, as he is still legally married to Arabella. Thus, after rebounding from this second bout with depression, he resolves upon the "ecclesiastical and altruistic life" as a licentiate, hoping to find therein a cure for his "modern vice of unrest." Jude feeds this latest aspiration by reading the Church Fathers, as well as Paley and Butler, and embarks upon what Sue later sniggeringly calls his "Tractarian stage" by reading Newman, Pusey, and other modern theological lights. He rounds out his training by practicing chants and studying religious art.

But Jude is too analytical not to recognize—and too honest to deny—that Sue matters most in his life. Having idealized her, Jude permits Sue to displace the Christian God within his life and henceforth turns to Sue to satisfy his basic needs for "something to love" and "some kind of hope to support" him. The nocturnal burning and burial of his theological tracts (p. 234) signals the futility of his ecclesiastical aspirations. After considering the "ethical contradictoriness" in cherishing an "unlicensed tenderness" for Sue while preparing to become a Christian soldier-servant, Jude acknowledges he is "as unfit, obviously, by nature, as . . . by social position, to fill the part of propounder of accredited dogma." When Sue leaves Phillotson to join Jude, he tells her that "the Church is no more to me. Let it lie! I am not to be one of

> 'The soldier-saints who, row on row,
> Burn upward each to his point of bliss,'

if any such there be! My point of bliss is not upward but here."[6]

If Christminster proves no anchor for Jude, Sue is no more reliable. The dreamer fell in love with her photograph, and it takes a long period of suffering, after he meets her, before he is stripped of his illusions. A haloed figure, associated with chaste mythological goddesses, Sue represents a superhuman type for Jude. Referring to her as "almost a divinity," Jude describes her in such terms as "ethereal," "uncarnate," "aerial," and "phantasmal, bodiless creature." Intellectual and independent, Sue seems to Jude a free thinker, delighting to be "outside all laws except gravitation and germination." She is an early instance of the "New Woman" of the 1890s. Ironically, however, Sue's physical attractiveness and accessibility undermine Jude's faith by exposing her perverse enslavement to the social and moral conventions of the time.

Jude's proclivity for violating his best interests is most evident in his relations with Sue. First, in seeking her out, he overcomes the counsel of his conscience and flouts the risk of the hereditary family curse in marriage; her being his cousin, and descending from another branch of the family with an unfortunate marital history, compounds the risks. Then, when he begins his pursuit—with its torturous sequence of approaches and separations, her impulsive invitations and fickle dismissals—Jude wonders if Sue is to break his heart, as she broke the heart of the young leader writer with whom she shared quarters previous to meeting Jude. Though he nearly starves himself to extinguish his passion for her and though Sue acknowledges he is like the martyr St. Stephen, Jude cannot separate himself from Sue, who remains his "God." His unconscious, self-sacrificial mission is revealed in the lines: "Crucify me, if you will! You know that you are all the world to me, whatever you do!" (p. 257).

Readers are not permitted to witness the short duration of their "natural marriage," when Jude and Sue celebrate their love in Greek joyousness. Presumably, however, Jude experiences the life-securing benefits of family society during this phase. Immunity from self-destructiveness is enhanced when he is able to give himself definitively to Sue and to hold her love securely. The increase in their family provides another powerful safeguard against suicide by giving greater order to his existence.[8] Even though Jude's prospects seem dimmed and his physical vigor declines, this is the fullest and happiest period of his life. In passing over it rapidly, Hardy maintains the essentially tragic tone of his fiction: he does not permit the joyousness to distract attention from Jude's inexorable movement toward his goal of self-destruction.

But if a sound "marriage" favors Jude by making him more immune to suicide than when he was separated from Sue, the devastation of their union after Little Father Time's hanging causes conjugal anomie and renews Jude's jeopardy.

Sue's hysterical reaction brings about what Jude calls her perverse "conversion" to Christianity, and Jude, who has been influenced by her earlier example and by her intellectual heroes to value pagan self-assertion, blames himself for Sue's fanatical self-denial.[9] By taking physical possession of Sue, Jude believes he has soiled the purity of his ideal. In one of the most poignant scenes in the novel, he expresses his guilt for despoiling his divinity:

> "I have seemed to myself lately," he said, "to belong to the vast band of men shunned by the virtuous—the men called seducers. It amazes me when I think of it! I have not been conscious of it or of any wrong-doing towards you, whom I love more than myself. Yet I am one of those men! . . . Yes, Sue—that's what I am. I seduced you. . . . You were a distinct type—a refined creature, intended by nature to be left intact. But I couldn't leave you alone!" [p. 352]

The self-accusing tone of this harangue is excessive and irrational. Jude knows that Sue's disturbance has been caused by forces beyond him and outside his control, and these condemnations recall his earlier judgments of himself as a "wicked worthless fellow" and "at bottom a vicious character." They represent a renewed effort by his guilt-driven, self-destructive instinct, "which had been his undoing more than once," to make him believe "that he was not worth the trouble of being taken care of either by himself or others" (p. 196).

As Sue prepares to abandon Jude, he is filled with forebodings. She has been his "social salvation," saving him from his uprooted condition and anchoring him to life, and she has been his source of hope, warding off threats of despair to which his too-sensitive, easily depressed nature has often made him prey. In melancholy madness, he beseeches his secular deity to preserve him from his "Arch

Enemies . . . my weakness for womankind and my impulse to strong liquor," the symbols of his loneliness and depression.

> "Don't abandon me to them, Sue, to save your own soul only! They have been kept entirely at a distance since you became my guardian angel! Since I have had you I have been able to go out into any temptations of the sort, without risk. Isn't my safety worth a little sacrifice of dogmatic principle? I am in terror lest, if you leave me, it will be with me another case of the pig that was washed turning back to his wallowing in the mire!" [p. 361]

Jude fears the consequences of deregulation of his married state.

Before Sue departs, Jude alludes to the account of Christ's death in Mark 15:35: "Then let the veil of our temple be rent in two from this hour!" We may interpret the rending as the severance of their union or the "death" of Sue, who has been Jude's hope and god throughout and who was earlier compared to Christ. Or we can read the allusion as a prophecy of the death of Jude, who has continuously manifested the Christlike virtue of loving-kindness.[10] In either case, he is henceforth without hope and love. Spiritually, Jude's life is over, sacrificed for the "fanatic prostitution" Sue is about to commit by returning to the bed of Phillotson. When he finally understands that her love for him has been reduced to fanatical compassion, to redeem his soul from sinfulness and suffering, Jude indignantly turns on Sue and cries: "Sue, Sue, you are not worth a man's love!" (p. 394). (A. Alvarez has claimed—rightly I believe—that the cry represents a standard of maturity and self-knowledge which Jude only slowly and painfully attains.)[11]

Throughout Jude's quest for self-knowledge and personal being, he is required to relinquish his ideals whenever they threaten his freedom to act as he believes he must. How-

ever, with his life continually deregulated, his ideas and
feelings constantly disturbed, Jude ultimately finds himself
in a "chaos of principles and emotions." Jude's faith in Sue
and Christminster, the idealized anchors for his soul, is
crushed by the grind of stern reality, and his resistance to
social pressures has made him reckless of continuing his life.
His anomie resurfaces when, in his "misery and depression"
at Sue's remarriage to Phillotson, "he turned into a public-
house for the first time during many months." Earlier, we
have seen that drink is an alternative form of self-destruction for Jude (for Henchard, it is a slower letting of his life's
blood). His aimlessness in life seems clearly expressed
"whenever he said 'I don't care what happens to me,' a thing
he did continually" (p. 381). Without Sue and his family,
without academic or ecclesiastical aspirations, Jude's will to
die is uncontested.

That he consciously seeks his death emerges in his frequent death wishes, however veiled they appear. For example, when he and Arabella pass the Martyr's burning place,
as she is preparing to ensnare Jude again, he recalls Dr.
Smith's sermon at the burning of Ridley: "*Though I give my
body to be burned, and have not charity, it profiteth me
nothing.*" Arabella, not understanding why Jude always
thinks of that passage when he passes this corner, is told,
"I'm giving my body to be burned!" (p. 382). Only weeks
after she has him under the padlock again (as she puts it),
Arabella complains about Jude's letting his health decline
and he replies that his greatest mercy would be to be killed
like the pig they slaughtered during their first union. And
after Arabella insults Sue to Jude's face, he threatens to kill
her "here and now! I've everything to gain by it—my own
death not being the least part" (p. 391).

Like Camus' Sisyphus, Jude is conscious that his torture
and suffering are permanent conditions; he can no longer

hope for any kind of success or anyone's love. When death seems clearly a gain, he risks his life by journeying to see Sue one last time: traveling in a "driving rain," the sick man "ventured out to almost certain death." Imaged as a walking corpse, he is described as "oddly swathed, pale as a monumental figure in alabaster," his face showing the determined purposes that alone sustain him. As he later tells Arabella, who is nearly incredulous that he meant to commit suicide ("Well, I'm blest! Kill yourself for a woman"):

> "I made up my mind that a man confined to his room by inflammation of the lungs, a fellow who had only two wishes left in the world, to see a particular woman, and then to die, could neatly accomplish those two wishes in one stroke by taking this journey in the rain. That I've done. I have seen her for the last time, and I've finished myself—put an end to a feverish life which ought never to have been begun!" [p. 397]

Back in Christminster, after his final, painful meeting with Sue, the "deadly chill . . . began to creep into his bones." Jude is satisfied that he has finished himself. His bitter knowledge of what it means to be Jude Fawley causes him to curse his unnecessary life. Defiantly. Quoting the bitter words of Job, Jude dies unattended while Arabella stalks her next victim amid the hurrahing Christminster undergraduates.

But for all the bitterness and pain in this tragic ending, there is an unmistakable sense in which Jude's suicide is heroic. A peculiarly modern *and* ancient character, Jude gives an essential clue to his death's quality in his last quotation from Job. Embracing death, he says:

> *"There the prisoners rest together; they heard not the voice of the oppressor. . . . The small and the great are there; and the servant*

is free from his master. Wherefore is light given to him that is in
misery, and life unto the bitter in soul?" [p. 408]

In Jude's education about himself, he has learned that
certain passions tend to master him—turn him into a slave.
But tutored by Sue and her intellectual heroes, Shelley,
Mill, and von Humboldt, and appalled by Sue's capitulation
to social codes and religious dogma, freedom has become for
him, finally, an overriding value. When he can commit
himself freely to the persons and purposes which are crucial
to his being, he can keep his archenemies under control.
But when he is deprived of hope, love, and even liberty,
Jude is too much the pagan to sustain a life of painful
enslavement. The implications of Jude's paganism dramatically influence one's critical perspective about his suicide.
In terms of a pagan ethos, Jude's act of self-destruction may
be seen as a heroic affirmation of his personal being.

A cluster of images in the novel pertains to paganism, and
their importance for Jude's character is considered by Norman Holland, who demonstrates that, latent within him,
Jude carries the seeds of paganism.[12] Fawley, who earlier
aspired to become a Christian clergyman, undergoes a spiritual crisis and parts company with his doctrines. He rejects
the ideals of Christianity, heavenly bliss and reward in the
afterlife, to search for worldly bliss in the present life. Jude
is converted to Sue's pagan views at the same time that Sue
is converted to Christianity. This exchange of positions between Jude and Sue gives a symmetrical structure to the
plot but, more importantly, it symbolizes the novel's rejection of Christian self-denial and its affirmation of pagan self-
assertion. When Sue's embrace of dogmatic Christianity
leads her to mortify her flesh and preach self-abnegation

and self-renunciation, Jude "rejects Christian self-denial, which he sees as hysterical, fanatic, perverse, in favor of Pagan self-assertion."[13] Ironically, Jude learns to value self-assertion from one of Sue's intellectual heroes, John Stuart Mill, who in *On Liberty* refutes the Calvinistic doctrine that man's great offense is self-will: "There is a different type of human excellence from the Calvinistic; a conception of humanity as having its nature bestowed on it for other purposes than merely to be abnegated. 'Pagan self-assertion' is one of the elements of human worth, as well as 'Christian self-denial.'"[14]

Tutored by Sue and Mill, Jude develops beyond the altruism that compelled him to marry Arabella. He grows to realize that the denial of self-will runs counter to his quest for personal being. For him, such a denial ultimately becomes the great sin, leading to forfeiture of personality and ending in enslavement. His paganism, which encourages his independent way of life, is based on the principle that man's point of bliss is here on earth. Denial of will has no part in Jude's pagan character, but Jude has given up all his external ideals and desires, and all he has known is suffering. Alone in the world, Jude learns that to be Jude Fawley, a free man, means to be frustrated, to be lonely, and to suffer. He stares into the void; then despairs.

But Jude is not defeated; his freedom is not forfeited; his death is not the result of determinism or cowardice. Søren Kierkegaard, like Hardy, a brilliant analyst of the spiritual ills of the modern world, treats despair in a way that illuminates the meaning of Jude's death:

> One cannot despair at all without willing it, but to despair truly one must truly will it, but when one truly wills it one is truly beyond despair; when one has truly willed despair one has truly chosen that which despair chooses, *i.e.*, oneself in one's eternal

validity. The personality is tranquillized only in despair, not by necessity, for I never despair by necessity, but by freedom, and only thereby does one win the absolute.[15]

Jude's despair is defiant and he has freely chosen it. Rather than capitulate to the enslaving forces that sought to strip away his freedom, Jude defies them. His defiance "really is despair by the aid of the eternal, the despairing abuse of the eternal in the self to the point of being despairingly determined to be oneself." Defiance "is not willing to begin by losing itself but wills to be itself." Kierkegaard gives this type of despair a name: "If one would have a common name for this despair, one might call it Stoicism—yet without thinking only of this philosophic sect."[16]

If we view his despair as a freely chosen act of the pagan Jude (as I believe we must), it can be seen as an act of self-assertion. Jude's awareness that to continue living means to continue suffering leads him to choose no longer to live. Terrible though this choice is, it is thoroughly authentic. For the pagan, as Hardy noted in his reading of "The Ethics of Suicide," there is no weakness or evil in the loss of life. Marcus Aurelius suggests that the good man is to approach death "pure, tranquil, ready to depart, and without any compulsion perfectly reconciled to his lot."[17] Evil for man is living in necessity; "yet there is no necessity for us to live in necessity: since Nature hath been so kind as to give us, though but one door into the world, yet many doors out of it."[18] Epicurus not only condones suicide but even recommends it in extreme cases, where suffering and misery are intolerable or calamity is inevitable. In such cases, "Self-homicide is an Act of Heroick Fortitude."[19] Epicurus writes:

But, albeit there be some Cases so extream, as that in respect of them we are to hasten and fly to the Sanctuary of Death, lest

some power intervene and rob us of that liberty of quitting life;
yet nevertheless are we not to attempt anything in that kind, but
when it may be attempted conveniently and opportunely; and
when that time comes, then are we to dispatch and leap over the
battlements of life bravely. For, neither is it fit for him, who
thinks of flight to sleep: nor are we to despair of a happy Exit
even from the greatest difficulties, in case we neither hasten
before our time, nor let it slip when it comes.[20]

It is significant that the last words Jude whispers—all
from the Book of Job—are a curse on his birth and a wish
that he had "given up the ghost" as soon as he emerged from
the womb; for then he would have been free, without
having to suffer throughout his life. It was his misfortune to
be given "light" in his misery, for his consciousness of his
suffering has made it more difficult to endure. Jude's final
words, nevertheless, represent the tragic discovery of the
novel; and it is at this time, when he understands fully the
meaning of his life, that he chooses to die. His choice is an
assertion that only the free life is worth living and that man
can live freely even to the end of his life.

Jude the Obscure provides a synthesis of Hardy's modern
ethical insights. Hardy explored the situation of man in the
modern world—an alienated, isolated consciousness confronting the void created by the absence of God. Man's
search for meaning becomes a search for himself, for he
alone is able to impose meaning on the disordered universe.
But his quest for self-realization requires freedom of will and
action, freedom of choice, and freedom from the various
enslaving elements within himself and his environment.

The vision of man projected in the novel through Jude
Fawley resembles the existential personality described by
the Russian theologian Nicholas Berdyaev, a type of charac-

ter who appears in the works of the great existentialist authors.

> The entire world is nothing in comparison with human personality, with the unique person of a man, with his unique fate. Man lives in an agony, and he wants to know where he is, where he comes from and whither he is going. . . . It is possible for man to get knowledge of himself from above or from below, either from his own light, the divine principle that is within him, or from his own darkness, the elemental subconscious demonic principle within him. And he can do this because he is a twofold and contradictory being. He is a being who is polarized in the highest degree, God-like and beast-like, exalted and base, free and enslaved, apt both for rising and for falling, capable of great love and kindness, capable also of great cruelty and unlimited egoism. Dostoyevsky, Kierkegaard and Nietzsche recognized the tragic principle in man and the inconsistency of his nature with peculiar distinctness.[21]

To Berdyaev's list, one might well add Thomas Hardy.

Because Jude Fawley despairs and commits suicide does not mean that Hardy sees no meaning for man in the modern world. *Jude* is a tragic novel in which Hardy exacts a full look at the worst situation that modern man faces. That many of the social ills and personal violations in the novel are remediable and, with the remedies of life, can be made less painful, cannot be overlooked. But these ills, which increase man's misery, threaten his freedom, and thwart his self-development, are merely the tragic machinery of the novel and secondary in importance to Jude Fawley's personal being. As Jacques Barzun stated long ago, "No reform of the divorce laws or the entrance requirements of Oxford would by itself alter the chances of . . . Jude's coming to happier ends."[22]

There remain the irremediable ills, the permanent facts of pain, suffering, and death. Amid these irremediable ills, Jude symbolizes man's quest for personal being through his defiant insistence upon personal freedom.

Altruistic Suicides

CHAPTER EIGHT

Giles Winterborne:
The Intensity of His Contrition

T H E R E A R E M A N Y indications that by the time Thomas
Hardy began to write *The Woodlanders*, late in 1885, he had
come of age as a novelist. He had always aspired to be more
than merely "a good hand at a serial,"[1] and with at least four
masterpieces behind him, he was in the front rank of England's living novelists. Since his return to Dorset and his
installation at Max Gate, Hardy had realized the practical
benefits of exploiting his deep understanding of his native
region, its people and their traditions, for his artistic productions. Sharing his century's conviction of the interdependence of the lives and work of all members in a
community, Hardy represented that interdependence by
the figure of a great web, a metaphor that occurs in a
notebook entry written while Hardy was preparing *The
Woodlanders*, and it appears in a famous passage in the
novel. Ruminating on the apparently isolated lives of Giles
and Marty South as they walk to work in the lonely pre-
dawn, the narrator remarks: "And yet their lonely courses
formed no detached design at all, but were part of the
pattern in the great web of human doings then weaving in

both hemispheres from the White Sea to Cape Horn" (*W*, p. 53).

Hardy's self-confidence as a novelist is manifested in his growing self-consciousness about his art and his exploration for new techniques. The notebook entries for late 1885 and early 1886, just after Hardy decided to go back to the original plot for his woodland story, reveal the concerns which were to account for, among other things, his characterization of Giles Winterborne. Early in 1886 he wrote: "*3 January:* My art is to intensify the expression of things . . . so that the heart and inner meaning is made vividly visible." Several months later, acknowledging that novel writing had become analytical, Hardy asked if novels cannot render "as visible essences, spectres, etc., the abstract thoughts of the analytic school?" This antirealistic aim, so much more appropriate for poetic than fictional art, was carried out most effectively in the Spirits of *The Dynasts*. There, too, the human race is shown as "one great network or tissue which quivers in every part when one point is shaken, like a spider's web when touched." But in *The Woodlanders*, Hardy's effort to render "the true realities of life, hitherto called abstractions," led him to his conception of the "Unfulfilled Intention," an abstract formulation which nevertheless accounts for the frustration of man's best-laid plans, the futility of his most cherished hopes. This idea, which is to figure in all the later novels, is presented as Melbury and Grace walk through the woods: "Here, as everywhere, the Unfulfilled Intention, which makes life what it is, was as obvious as it could be among the depraved crowds of a city slum. The leaf was deformed, the curve was crippled, the taper was interrupted; the lichen ate the vigour of the stalk, and the ivy slowly strangled to death the promising sapling" (p. 82). What is startling about this novel is its perception of the violent struggle for survival in society as well as in nature. Human beings and their intentions are as vulnerable to social and psychological forces as plants and saplings are to lichens and ivy.

Hardy's images of deformity, destruction, and death heighten our sense of the essentially tragic nature of his vision of the Unfulfilled Intention; hence his claim of a Sophoclean character for his woodland drama[2] and his redefinition of tragedy, within days after resuming his original plot for *The Woodlanders*, to incorporate the idea of the Unfulfilled Intention. He wrote on November 21–22, 1875: "Tragedy. It may be put thus in brief: a tragedy exhibits a state of things in the life of an individual which unavoidably causes some natural aim or desire of his to end in a catastrophe when carried out" (*L*, p. 176).

Within the tightly integrated woodlands community of Little Hintock, Hardy set his latest variation on the conflict between nature and civilization. In *The Woodlanders*, the chief victim of the Unfulfilled Intention is Giles Winterborne. Inhabiting a world where the struggle for survival is everywhere apparent, Giles is endangered when his natural aim, to marry the superficially cultivated Grace Melbury, is thwarted. Able to read nature's alphabet and speak in "the tongue of the trees and fruits and flowers themselves," Giles suffers because of his entanglement in the great web of society—whose animus against the individual, as has been seen, was Hardy's obsessive theme in his later fictions.[3] The familiar trio of lovers who shape the plots and create the conflicts in so many Hardy novels are again brought forward in the region of the Hintocks: the faithful, diffident, but persistent man of the country; his socially superior, flashy, more worldly, and sexually aggressive rival from the outside world; and their charming but willful and provokingly inconstant well-beloved. As the novel begins, there is good reason to expect Giles's intention to be ful-

filled: his claim to Grace seems solidly founded on their
youthful affection for one another and her father's determination to hasten their union as an act of expiation for having
cheated Giles's father in a love contest.

The "pressure of events," however, interferes and over-
turns both Melbury's and nature's striving to join Grace and
Giles (W, p. 291). Melbury's social ambitions, which are far
more powerful and compelling than his moral conscience,
cause him to educate Grace for a "fortunate" marriage, as he
perceives her as both the instrument of his revenge against
the despised aristocrats, who scorned his ignorance, and
the lever for raising his family to the same rung as his "social
betters." So when Grace returns from her schooling, she
seems to her father too precious to "throw away" on Giles.
Moreover, Melbury's anxious temporizing over the match is
perpetuated by Grace's indecisive nature and filial affection,
which make ineffective her early resistance of her father's
perverse aims.[4] Though she is uncomfortable bearing the
family's hope for social advancement, her innocent roman-
ticizing of the Lady at the Great House exposes her own
social pretensions. Ironically, she seems to support and
strengthen her father's aversion to the marriage with Giles,
for she is enough affected by the veneer of cultivation she
had attained among her classmates to feel uncomfortable
with, and superior to, Giles.

The most decisive pressure, of course, comes when
Fitzpiers alights in the woodlands and shakes the great
web, finally rending it before he moves on. A dilettante
descended from an ancient family, Fitzpiers dabbles in scientific experiments, metaphysics, and Romantic poetry. To
the woodland rustics, linked together by hard work in a
battle for survival, Fitzpiers' exotic activities suggest he has
made a pact with the devil. His original pursuit of Grace,
which begins in boredom and is nourished by the "recrea-

tive character of such acquaintance" (p. 157), identifies the debased Faust as a heartless brother of Dickens' Jem Harthouse.[5] Still, for the pretentious George Melbury, Fitzpiers possesses all the advantages of an ancient name and high connections; if his family's fortunes have lapsed and the doctor is impoverished, Melbury is quite willing to supply Fitzpiers' deficiencies. Through Grace's marriage to Fitzpiers, whose influence over her emotions resembles Mop Ollamoor's demonic possession of Car'line Aspent in Hardy's story "The Fiddler of the Reels," Melbury wishes to achieve his social dreams.

In the primitive world of the woodlands, the individual's life is rigorously governed by custom and habit. Where everyone leads the same kind of life, the ideas, feelings, and occupations common to nearly all the members create a powerful form of collective supervision over the individual; and the effects of customary social forces are indicated early in *The Woodlanders*. Not only are such respectable members of the community as Giles and John South dependent on Mrs. Charmond for their living and dwelling, but even so humble a person as Marty South must indulge the lady's fancy if she requires so personal a possession as Marty's hair. In Giles's case, the price one pays for violating the prerogatives of one's superiors is loss of his financial and social standing, and with them his hopes for marrying Grace. Because he would not defer to Mrs. Charmond at the encounter of his timber carriage and her vehicle, Giles ultimately loses his unsecured lifehold properties. Even though reason and justice are on his side, Mrs. Charmond refuses to recognize his moral right to retain his holdings for life. Because he is "unfortunate in his worldly transactions"—as Grace puts it when she compares Giles to Hamlet's friend, who "in suffering all . . . suffers nothing" (p. 238)—it is easier for

George Melbury to justify not "wasting" his daughter on Giles and uniting her with Fitzpiers.

The individual's lack of personal value and his vulnerability to the collective will in the primitive woodland society are most vividly revealed when Giles is encouraged to renew his courtship of Grace, who soon expects to be divorced from her philandering husband. Giles accepts the responsibility to exercise "the necessary care not to compromise Grace by too early advances" (p. 291), and her "wish to keep the proprieties" as well as she can, even though she believes she is no longer morally bound to Fitzpiers, becomes an inviolable law for Giles. But when Grace realizes the full extent of Giles's chivalrous fidelity, she deplores her selfish correctness and asks if "cruel propriety" is killing "the dearest heart that ever woman clasped to her own!" (p. 324).

Certainly, "cruel propriety" contributes to Giles's "strange self-sacrifice" (p. 325), as does Melbury's social ambition and Mrs. Charmond's thoughtless disregard for Giles's moral right to his properties. All of these social pressures, which set limits on individuality and subordinate one's personal worth to false social values, activate Giles's tendency to martyrdom and increase his vulnerability to self-destruction. But social forces alone cannot account for Giles's "altruistic suicide" (as Durkheim would describe it).[6] For Giles, as for all Hardy's suicides, his character effects his fate. Although the nature of Giles's death differs from Henchard's, as a faithful martyr's differs from an outcast Cain's, both reflect a death instinct too powerful to be withstood.

With "reserve in his glance, and restraint upon his mouth," Giles Winterborne makes his first appearance in the novel (p. 53). A lover and a person of affairs, Giles is not in the habit of regarding his inner self spectacularly; as a result, he fails to note the rare power he possesses: that of keeping both judgment and emotion suspended in difficult cases. In this he is very much like Gabriel Oak at the start of *Far from the Madding Crowd*,[7] but Giles's self-repression and underestimation of himself are far more fatal than Oak's unassuming demeanor.

Hardy permits Giles to show his essentially self-defeating, self-destructive nature in his first important encounter with Grace, whose father has decided to encourage their marrying. At their reunion when Grace returns home from school, Giles reacts to the "restrained shape" of her greeting: his rough appearance causes his initial awkwardness, as Grace looks "glorified and refined to much above her former level." Now Giles certainly understands the importance of his opportunity to welcome Grace back home, and it is no exaggeration to say that his chief reason for being is to marry Grace. Also, he realizes that a woman's opinion of a man may be influenced by such "non-essentials" as "the colour of a hat, the fold of a coat, the make of a boot." But he refuses to act on his reflections because of "a certain causticity of mental tone towards himself and the world in general." The "causticity" figure is most suggestive here, for there is a corrosive quality about Giles's refusal to act with a lover's enthusiasm—a mordant unwillingness to preen himself to attract and flatter his mate. Nor is this "laxness," as the narrator judges it, unusual; rather, his lack of self-importance prevents enthusiasm "as always." Equally characteristic is Giles's gloomy reaction to disappointing Grace, whom he idealizes (one is tempted to say "idolizes") far more intensely than Fitzpiers does (p. 68).

Giles's profound lack of self-esteem repeatedly comes to the surface, early and late. It appears when Giles indulges in "self-derision" because the Melburys, excited at Grace's return, forget about him after he delivers their daughter (p. 76). When he wants to "bring matters to a point" between Grace and himself, "his self-deprecatory sense of living on a much smaller scale than the Melburys" leads to the damaging failure of his Christmas party (p. 97). Later, after Melbury confides to him the failure of Grace's marriage and says that Giles ought to have had her, the lacerated young man undervalues himself as not sufficiently educated, too rough, and too poor to make Grace happy (p. 245). Even when Grace and her father encourage Giles to marry her after her expected divorce, his determination to humble himself and his way of living provoke Grace to insist that he willfully misunderstands her affection for him (p. 298). The frustrated young woman seems to have an acute understanding of his unconscious will. Finally, his susceptibility to Grace's social tastes, however superficial and transitory, spoil even the most promising moments for Giles, so that, in thinking over the unsatisfactory ending of a pleasant time, he forgets the pleasant time itself.

That Giles is responsible for causing many of his own injuries cannot be denied, even in the instances where he unwittingly or unconsciously harms himself. In his relations with George Melbury and Mrs. Charmond, Giles precipitates his misfortunes by acting in a way that disserves his best interests, for his preoccupation with the vagaries of his romance with Grace causes him to subvert that rare power in him: his ability to keep judgment and emotion suspended in trying cases. Such a lapse occurs in the auction scene, where Giles's two roles as lover and man-of-affairs come into conflict. Watching the snowflakes descend on his well-beloved's hair, Giles is distracted and his attention to business slackens as he wanders mentally "in an abstracted mood," and he is unaware that his incoherent bidding against Grace's father is creating a dangerous tension between them

(p. 84). Later, the father's reluctance to "throw Grace away" on Giles is reinforced at the Christmas party, where once again Giles's inattention to domestic niceties results in frustration. His "muddling style of housekeeping" and "the sort of society" he imposed on the Melburys could not but offend Grace's pretentious father. Even Grace, who is determined not to be displeased, depressed Giles with her "kindly pity of his household management." The result of Giles's lack of tact, of course, is to weaken Melbury's resolutions to see the pair united. In a prophetic tone, the narrator comments on Giles's half-unconscious dining: "He could not get over the initial failures in his scheme for advancing his suit" (pp. 98–105).

The damage Giles does to his marriage plans, moreover, is paralleled by his undercutting of his social and financial position. As a landholder, Giles is never completely secure, since both his father and he neglected the simple legal formality to preserve the Winterborne properties for the duration of Giles's life. Thus if the last person Giles should offend is his future father-in-law, the last person he should alienate is Mrs. Charmond, into whose possession Giles's homestead and cottages will descend upon John South's death. But Giles's habit of speaking his mind (when he speaks at all), which keeps him from being an effective salesman of his trees and cider, proves disastrous in the collision and confrontation over his and Mrs. Charmond's carriages. His adamant refusal to defer to her coachman shows Giles making an uncharacteristically emotional judgment. Robert Creedle tallies the price of Giles's rigidity when he reminds the young man that his reckless defiance of Mrs. Charmond lost his houses for him (p. 133).

It is only fair to acknowledge that Giles is as much the victim of Melbury's social ambitions and Mrs. Charmond's irresponsible selfishness as he is of his own failures to ad-

vance his suit and secure his foothold in Little Hintock, but
it is in his pursuit of Grace that his lack of self-esteem is
most insidious. The superbly impressionistic scene, where
Giles is "shrouding" John South's tree before felling it,
evokes his fatal ineffectiveness as a lover. Even before he
discovers Grace's determination to obey her father's wish
not to see him again, Giles is shown climbing a ladder to
begin his work and "cutting away his perches as he went."
Thus Hardy's symbolic presentation of Giles looks back to
his alienation of Melbury and forward to his encounter with
Mrs. Charmond. At Grace's repeated rebuffs, he proceeds
"automatically with his work" and climbs higher into the
sky, "cutting himself off more and more from all intercourse
with the sublunary world." But when Grace approaches to
tell Giles, plainly and candidly, that they must not think too
much of the "engagement, or understanding, between us,"
Giles's only reaction is to reply that he has nothing to say
until he has thought a while. He remains in the tree, resting
with his head on his hand, an embodiment of despair, until
"the fog and the night had completely inclosed him from her
view" (p. 122). The novel's themes of loneliness and sterility
are nowhere more apparent than in this image of Giles's self-
enclosure in the fogs of Niflheim.

Hardy's narrator immediately raises the question: What
would have happened if Giles had descended the tree to
confront Grace? The probabilities, he decides, are that
Giles might have overcome her filial, acquiescent frame of
mind. The narrator apparently shares the opinion of a
woman Hardy knew, who declared that "one of their sex is
never so much inclined to throw in her lot with a man for
good and all as five minutes after she has told him such a
thing cannot be."[8] More authoritatively and more to the

point, Grace tells Giles, after the first and only time he kisses her: "Giles, if you had only shown half the boldness before I married that you show now, you would have carried me off for your own, first instead of second" (p. 304). But though Grace waited on the ground, Giles "continued motionless and silent in that gloomy Niflheim or fogland which involved him." Literally, his unnatural repression of his emotions is a fatal mistake.

Giles's "lack of perseverance" as a lover seems to Grace the only defect in his otherwise perfect character. It surfaces again when, after Mrs. Charmond refuses to extend Giles's lease, he is discouraged from his suit by Marty's prophetic couplet:

> O Giles, you've lost your dwelling-place.
> And therefore, Giles, you'll lose your Grace.

Even though only hours ago he had decided to learn his fate from Grace herself, Marty's lines "decided the question for him." He relinquishes his claim to Grace because of his "terrible belief" that Marty's prophecy is turning out to be true, despite his efforts to regain Grace. But clearly, Giles's belief goes counter to the reality of Grace's feelings. Giving in so easily to what he believes is his fate is ironic, as Giles does not see Grace rub out Marty's "lose" and insert "keep"—a sign of her "warming to more sympathy" with Giles (p. 136).

Giles's failure to persevere in his suit for Grace is dramatized in the scene on Midsummer Night, where Fitzpiers seizes and wins the prize that Giles is too indifferent to claim. Inevitably, in *The Woodlanders* as in *Far from the Madding Crowd*, the diffident countryman, who so idealizes his lover as to prevent himself from reaching out to take her, loses his woman to the experienced outsider who exploits his sexual mastery. And where Fitzpiers tries to dominate Grace's impulses and shape "her will into passive concurrence with all his desires," Giles is too honorable, "too straightforward to influence her further against her better judgment," even when mere propriety is at issue (p. 296). It is simply the case—as so often in Hardy—that the more noble character is the less effective lover.

Eventually, Giles loses Grace *and* his properties, but unlike Gabriel Oak, whom he resembles in many ways, Giles does not learn from his failures. He does not bounce back, with a vital spring, to ensure that remediable ills and dangers do not overcome him again.[9] Rather, he resembles Henchard in repeatedly failing in precisely those endeavors and relationships that mean everything to him. Both men are so intent on failing that, paradoxically, they can realize themselves only by sacrificing their lives.

Giles's self-sacrifice begins when he starts to withdraw from life after Grace tells him they must end their agreement to marry. His symbolic cutting away of his perches isolates him from the world while his climbing upward puts him in the motionlessness, silence, and gloom of Niflheim, the Scandinavian realm of death—the empty abyss where cold freezes the sinews and paralyzes the will. Hardy's allusion to the Norse equivalent of hell foreshadows his hero's mortal illness, and in describing Giles's severance from Grace as "more like a burial of her than a rupture," he intuits the intimate relationship that Freud would later describe between mourning and melancholia.[10] In the classical fashion of melancholiacs, Giles feels the chill come over his soul and enter his veins as his heart lies in the grave with Grace, who is virtually dead to him. Soon "a distracting regret for his loss" of Grace is compounded by the loss of his worldly fortune; and from that day onward, Giles "retired into the background of human life and action" (p. 137).

Though Giles continues to love Grace, there is something bloodless in that love—something that keeps him from expressing passion for her. The "off-hand manner of indifference" which had grown upon him makes him back off in disdain when Fitzpiers steps forward and captures Grace in his arms on Midsummer Night; and his neighbors notice that "a certain laxity had crept into his life," a "cynical gaze" into his eyes. His wandering around the pulled-down homestead, the narrator suggests, reveals a feeling that "might have been called morbid" (pp. 170, 195, 206).

The effects of Giles's melancholia are apparent in the scene where he is working outside the hotel where Grace is spending her honeymoon. Robert Creedle has just catalogued what he has lost "through your letting slip she that was once your own!" And to add to his misery, Grace calls down to Giles, moiling and muddling for his daily bread, and opens his old wounds in her thoughtless pride of life. Reduced to uncharacteristic self-pity, he recoils upon her with unreasoning anger, reproaching her bitterly; but—and here is the wonder of Hardy's psychological penetration—in the next moment a far more tender mood ensues, in which Giles "could regard her renunciation of such as he as her glory and her privilege, his own fidelity notwithstanding." This glorification of Grace and Giles's self-degradation are reinforced by the poem to which the narrator alludes in describing Giles's feeling:

> You filled my barren life with treasure;
> You may withdraw the gift you gave,
> You still are queen, I still am slave,
>   Though you forget. [p. 200]

Something seems amiss here. Giles has had to make the sternest renunciation, and his fidelity to Grace is much finer than her feeling of superiority over him. When, one must ask, did Grace "fill" Giles's barren life, and with what "treasure," what "gift"? Why is she permitted to "withdraw" her gift, to "forget"? Clearly, Giles's self-destructiveness has found its direction, has been canalized by his loss of Grace through her death to him. Like a mourning lover, he has idealized her, demeaned himself before her, and is preparing to sacrifice himself to her.[11] Thus, though his "queen" may forget him,

> May I sink meanlier than the worst,
> Abandoned, outcast, crushed, accurst, —
> If I forget. [p. 199]

The violence of this language recalls the self-destructive mission of Henchard after he finally "lost" Elizabeth-Jane. With profound insight, Hardy makes us see how Giles's reproaches against himself, his implicit accusations and violent threats, are not warranted by his actions toward Grace, though they might be warranted by Grace's having forgotten Giles. In the ambivalence of his feelings at the moment, he is conscience stricken for having reproached the woman he idolizes, even though she deserves reproach. But because he cannot permit himself to attack her, he will turn his vehemence upon himself. His actions represent an effort to displace his anger against his beloved; his self-reproaches result from reproachful feelings against Grace, which have been shifted back upon himself.[12]

In this impressive scene, Giles reveals all the instincts of a martyr. His fidelity to the idealized Grace and his capacity for self-commitment to her, even to the extent of self-sacrifice, are disturbingly clear. Momentary self-pity exposes his loss of self-respect, and this allows him both to forgive Grace's forgetfulness and, expressing the feelings of the speaker in Gosse's poem, insist on her queenliness—in complete disregard of the realities of their relationship. The poem's other petitions for abandonment, crushing, cursing, represent, implicitly, Giles's death wish. So abject is the unfortunate lover that he evokes Irving Howe's famous lament: "No one, neither man nor dog, should have to be that loyal." Giles, it seems to Howe, is "vexed by aspirations to saintliness."[13]

Giles's momentary infidelity in this scene prefigures the crucial violation later, where the occasion for sacrificing himself is prepared. Again, her father's manipulation of Grace's life renews the pair's intention to be wed. Melbury's pressure on Grace to give Giles "some temporary encouragement, even though it is over-early," leads to their meeting in Sherton Abbey to consider their future together. Giles is now able to criticize Grace, although "Time had been when to criticize a single trait in Grace Melbury would have lain as far beyond his powers as to criticize a deity." He finds her "better, much better" than she used to be, and is grieved that he had criticized her. The habit of idealization, it seems, has taken hold and hardened in Giles, but Grace's greater dignity, ideas, assurance—as Giles judged them— are ironically undercut by her description (with him) as "arcadian innocents," "children in the presence of the incomprehensible." And her emotional uncertainty and social fastidiousness are apparent in her worries over "seeming rather fast" in letting him hold her hand in the abbey, the divorce papers being as yet unsigned. Grace's wish to keep the proprieties not only overcomes Giles's desire to give her "one poor little kiss," in case one of them should die before the divorce becomes final; it even chastises him into repentance for pouring out his heart to her.

In imagining Giles's reaction to their reunion, Hardy achieves a profound intimation of the man's tortured emotions. Grace had noticed, in speaking of the time's being premature for lovemaking, "something in his brain of the nature of an enemy to her." Could his presentiment of an early death bring those lines into his forehead, or unconscious reaction to her heartlessness in putting propriety before his heart's desperate worship of her? For all the sympathy Grace develops for Giles, her uncertainty about expressing it exacerbates both his suffering and guilt; and both inevitably feed his self-destructive nature. Thus, rather than criticize Grace, Giles abuses himself for being "hopelessly blind to propriety," for blundering in ordering Grace's lunch in a humble tavern, and for not seeing that "what was good enough for me was not good enough" for her (pp. 294–98). Though Grace's behavior is far from blameless, at the scene's end she is rightly frustrated at Giles's apparently willful misunderstanding of her reactions.

When Giles leaves Grace, he is assaulted by doubts whether they could be happy together. Because he "had once worshipped her, laid out his life to suit her, wooed her, and lost her," he could not tread the old tracks again with the same hope. In determining not to move another step toward Grace, but to repulse her, Giles's thoughts and feelings are increasingly expressed in the religious language of repentance and sacrifice. The implicit self-destructiveness emerges explicitly as Giles takes on the character of a martyr and ascetic. Thus he will repulse her "as a tribute to conscience. It would be sheer sin to let her prepare a pitfall for her happiness not much smaller than the first by inveigling her into a union with such as he. Her poor father was now blind to these subtleties, which he had formerly beheld as in noontide light. It was his own duty to declare them— for her dear sake" (p. 299). For all its delusions, the passage is profoundly moving as it shows the inexorable logic with which Giles pushes himself towards his grave. Even Grace could sense in him "an air of determined abandonment of the whole prospect that lay in her direction."

There is something exceedingly insightful about Grace's fear of abandonment. The word itself recalls the curse that would befall Giles "If I forget." In fact, abandonment might be an appropriate penalty for one who forgets a lover, as Grace had forgotten Giles, even if he cannot consciously admit its appropriateness. Can it be, then, that Giles unconsciously abandons Grace while he consciously believes he is saving her from a second fall? Could this unconscious aim be what she feared in his silence, which seemed an enemy to her? It is possible that the underlying motive for his self-sacrifice is the unconscious aggression he displays in abandoning his idol. Nothing is more typical of the emotional ascetic than aggression, in the forms of disappointment and rejection, against his lover.[14]

Such a judgment seems more likely when we analyze Giles's curious reaction to Beaucock's letter. After the possibility of Grace's divorce is doomed, Giles is forced to "renounce her for ever." We should expect Giles to be relieved that circumstances intervened to reinforce his decision to repulse Grace and, as it were, for both of them, to take the sting out of having to give her up. Since it would be wrong to encourage her, and since they were not well suited (as he seems to have convinced himself), the enforced renunciation would seem a blessing in disguise, particularly for Grace's "dear sake." Not Giles, in effect, but the higher powers of the law are responsible.

But it is not at all in this mood that Giles receives the news. It now appears cruel, nearly tragic, that she could not be his. In his complex reaction, there is a terrible despair when he realizes that, finally, Grace is lost to him; and his deep and distracting love for her now reasserts itself. Moreover, he feels no satisfaction in her loss, not even in Grace's

being spared a second bad marriage. Nor, on the unconscious level, does he gain the satisfaction of retaliating in
kind against Grace for her original abandonment of him. In
disallowing the divorce, the law has seized his reason for
destroying himself, since the logical penalty for abandoning
her would be his self-abandonment. The insidious *lex talionis* cuts both ways, against Grace and Giles, in the
rigorous courtroom of Giles's conscience. Thus, required to
mourn her loss a second time, the melancholic Giles reacts
by "staring into the earth," declaring that his happiness can
only come when "the sun shines flat on the north front of
Sherton Abbey. That is, he can never again be happy above
the ground. And if the sting of separation is not removed, if
his aggression against Grace is displaced by that of the law,
if there is no offense, no guilt involved in the separation,
and no need for a suicidal reparation, then Giles must find
another cause for sacrificing himself.

Like an ascetic who seeks temptations to sin in order that
he may do greater penances, Giles seizes his opportunity in
the excruciating scene when Grace offers to let him kiss
her—only moments after he learns they cannot be married.
Giles's conscience becomes an arena in which his intense
longing "once in his life" to clasp Grace wars with his sense
of the enormity of "the wrong, the social sin," of taking
advantage of her lips. The language of the battleground
pervades the scene: his temptation approaches him "in
regular siege" as he "fight[s] valiantly against himself all this
while." The implications of his internal struggle, his violation of Grace's trust and "the household laws" by which he
has always lived, and his ignoring both past and future to
seize the "present and what it brought," are fatal. With this
one kiss, the war within him between his life and death
instincts is decided; for this one moment, he forfeits his self-
respect and his future (p. 303).

Immediately after the kiss, Giles begins to pay for his violation of Grace. Over and above his previous sorrows, he feels "like a very Cain," the first murderer. The allusion recalls both Henchard and Gosse's poem, where the speaker's penalty for forgetting his lover is to be "abandoned, outcast, crushed, accurst." The prophecy, it seems, has been fulfilled in Giles's sense of his sinful cruelty against Grace. Even so, his offense against her is so great that he cannot understand why he did it—how he could have dreamt of kissing her. Hardy's technique, the rhetorical question, suggests the ambivalence of Giles's motives, the psychological disturbance that attends the war within, and the ego's recoiling from a full look at the conscience's exactions.

The final stage in Giles's existence is the hopeless death-in-life he faces after he returns to his home. No one knows of Giles's serious illness, as he has withdrawn into a "suppressed and hidebound" routine for a while. In reparation for his one moment of pleasure, he adopts the ascetic's self-denial and refuses to send for a doctor, not thinking his case serious enough. But Hardy's narrator, who understands the dangerous relation between physical illness and spiritual desolation, notes that Giles's ailment "acquire[s] virulence with the prostration of his hopes" (p. 307). His insight anticipates by nearly half a century Menninger's elaboration of Freud's idea of "somatic compliance": "The possibility is that such infections become serious in just those cases where there are strongly active self-destructive tendencies. . . . It is possible that the available strengh of the death instinct determines this biological acceptance of the extraneous opportunities for self-destruction" (M, pp. 78–79).

When Grace seeks his help in her flight from Fitzpiers, she is a catalyst in mobilizing the self-destructive forces at work in Giles. He is, on the conscious level, the intensely contrite sinner, determined to clear his conscience and deserve her faith at last, even if it requires his martyrdom. The narrator's remark that, in offering his aid, Giles was "taxing a convalescence which could ill afford such self-sacrifice"(W, p. 313) couldn't be more explicit. It reveals the altruistic ascetic's determination to destroy the self by his self-imposed rigors.

Again on the conscious level, Giles's martyrlike behavior until his death is consistently generous to Grace and careless of himself. He accepts the physical agony of giving her his home while he retires to a cold, damp hut in the woods. And the "purity" of his affection arms him against repetition of his earlier "frailty." His knowledge that their crisis could end in nothing but sorrow is effaced by his triumphant thought that he is retrieving her trust. Thus his health disintegrates while Grace is hardly aware of the extent of his altruism. His refusal of food and shelter and his inability to sleep indicate how his instinct to cling to life has declined.

In the violent "devilry of a gusty night in a wood," Giles relinquishes his hold upon his hopeless life. Grace's recognition that she "was not worth such self-sacrifice" and her call to him, "*Come to me, dearest! I don't mind what they say or what they think of us any more*," are too late. Like a martyr, willing to die rather than compromise Grace again, Giles makes his choice: "He would not come in" (p. 321).

For some readers, Giles's refusal to enter the house is incredibly absurd. How, they ask, could a lover deny himself the erotic satisfaction he consciously seeks and needs, especially when his beloved implores him to come to her? Surely, there is something unnatural in Giles's restraint; but despite Hardy's unsophisticated technique, Giles's refusal is both credible and profoundly illuminating. An answer, suggested by psychology, is consistent with Grace's fear that

Giles bears some antagonism toward her. It may be that—
behind much that passes for love—there is much unconscious hatred. The iron control imposed by the ascetic Giles
over his sexual impulse, which is related to his chronic
passivity as a lover, may represent a kind of aggression by
one whose "love development" has been thwarted. By
means of this form of self-denial in pursuit of a higher goal
(namely, Grace's social respectability), Giles expresses his
aggression indirectly, making Grace's suffering appear incidental to his own greater martyrdom. In this way he man-
ages both to punish her and shift the responsibility for his
aggression from his conscience.[15] Thus, while it appears he
is martyring himself for the idealized virtue of Grace, his
refusal to join her may be his unconscious retaliation against
her earlier abandonment of him. The price he must pay for
that abandonment of his idol is, of course, his own life. With
his suicide, he gains the conscious satisfaction of martyring
himself and the unconscious satisfaction of releasing his
aggression against Grace.

When Grace finds Giles dying in his miserable hut, "her
prescient fear" over his welfare is realized. The word "prescient" brings to the reader's consciousness a disturbing idea
that has been lurking in the mind: the thought—suggested
by such descriptions of Grace as a "self-constituted nun," a
woman of "Daphnean instinct," with "more of Artemis than
of Aphrodite in her constitution"—that Grace is somehow
driving Giles to "this strange self-sacrifice." Has she not
earlier admitted "she should not have accepted it of him"?
The suspicion is strengthened by the narrator's chastising
Grace for underrating Giles's "chivalry till now, though she
knew him so well." Nor is this thought dispelled by her
reaction to the soaked martyr: "'O, my Giles,' she cried,
'what have I done to you!'" She sounds a deep note of
complex guilt when, impulsively covering him with useless

and tragically tardy kisses, she moans, "How could I! How could I!" (pp. 324–25).

Giles's death, then, is rife with ambiguity. As he is dying, he seems apotheosized in Grace's eyes for "the purity of his nature, his freedom from the grosser passions, his scrupulous delicacy." The burning brightness in his eyes and his acquiescence in all of Grace's labors suggest that he is already living in some visionary world. Like the altruistic suicide, for whom death is a means of union with a deity or loved one, he looks upon Grace as "some angel or other supernatural creature" (p. 325).[16] But her premature canonization of the martyr who "immolated himself for her comfort, cared more for her self-respect than she had thought of caring," raises real questions about the value of such an apparently generous and courageous martyrdom.

Does Giles's death serve any useful social purpose? Are Grace's comfort and self-respect worth dying for? What part do delusions about and aggression toward Grace play in Giles's self-destruction? And to what extent is he a victim, manipulated by Grace's cold, virginal aggressiveness? The novel's greatest irony may be that Giles's self-destructive nature is drawn inexorably to the man-destroying instincts of Grace Melbury, a prototype for Hardy's most notorious *femme fatale,* Sue Bridehead. Ultimately, his martyrdom seems achieved for personal satisfaction rather than for any social or spiritual good.

It could be argued that Giles's needless and wasteful death is a pointless sacrifice. His idolatry for Grace is exposed as a delusion, and his fidelity to the social proprieties demonstrates, in a profoundly pathetic way, the perversion of natural sexual impulses by the artificial codes of courtship and marriage. Still, for all the ambivalence surrounding Giles's self-destruction, the reader cannot but be moved by Hardy's penetrating awareness of what Mrs. Charmond calls "the extremes that people are capable of going to!"

CHAPTER NINE

Tess Durbeyfield:
"She Would Pay to the Uttermost
Farthing"

IN THE INTRODUCTION to a recent edition of *Tess of
the D'Urbervilles*, P. N. Furbank claimed that in "the clash
of Angel and Tess [Hardy] was dramatising the life-denying
and life-affirming elements in his own temperament. . . .
She represents, among so many other things, the natural
instinct of delight and truth of feeling, as against perversion." Whatever its validity as an analysis of Hardy, Furbank's observation directs attention to an essential matter in
the novel: the conflict between life-affirming and life-denying elements in Tess Durbeyfield.

Earlier critics, most notably Irving Howe, have celebrated Tess's "incomparable vibrancy and lovingness" and
her embodiment of "the inviolability of the person." Describing her as "one of the great images of human possibility," Howe sees Tess as "spontaneously committed to
the most fundamental needs of human existence." She provides, Howe says, "a standard of what is right and essential
for human beings to demand from life."[1]

Howe's conviction that Tess is among the greatest female
characters in literature is shared, of course, by many of

Hardy's readers, and his eloquent tribute to Hardy's conception of Tess "in the chaste, and chastening, spirit of the New Testament" goes to the heart of his achievement in this novel. Howe's enthusiasm over Tess's vibrancy is contagious and more than a little convincing—so that Furbank's contention that Tess is "life-affirming" seems all the more warranted, especially in view of the novel's elaboration of Hardy's evolving "pleasure principle." The narrator's comments on the "irresistible, universal, automatic tendency to find sweet pleasure somewhere" and the "invincible instinct towards self-delight" both relate to Tess as she overcomes her first great sufferings and begins her rally in "Phase the Third." Yet, for all the associations of Tess with pleasure and self-delight, we cannot ignore Hardy's awareness that the "appetite for joy" (which is nowhere more triumphantly and joyously presented than when Tess accepts Angel's proposal of marriage)[2] is always, and almost overwhelmingly, opposed by oppressive and victimizing forces.

I have previously noted—as tentative impressions in *The Mayor of Casterbridge* and *The Woodlanders*—Hardy's sense of a "life instinct" in conflict with a "death impulse," and in the *Life*, in notes made shortly before *Tess* was published, are further comments on Hardy's perception of this collocation of joy and suffering. In July of 1888, for example, Hardy "'Thought of the determination to enjoy. We see it in all nature, from the leaf on the tree to the titled lady at the ball. . . . It is achieved, of a sort, under superhuman difficulties. Like pent-up water it will find a chink of possibility somewhere. Even the most oppressed of men and animals find it, so that out of a thousand there is hardly one who has not a sun of some sort for his soul'" (*L*, p. 213). A few months later, on February 26, 1889, there is a cryptic note which may reflect Hardy's expressionistic impulses in his later novels and *The Dynasts*, namely, his determination to render the "abstract realisms" or the "true realities of life" as "visible essences" (*L*, p. 177). "In time one might get to regard every object, and every action, as composed, not of this or that material, this or that movement, but of the qualities pleasure and pain in varying proportions'" (*L*, p. 217). Significantly, the most explicit recognition of the opposed forces is in *Tess* itself, where the abandoned heroine has forgotten the injustice of her lot and indulges in pleasant memories of Talbothays with Marian. The narrator notes: "So the two forces were at work here as everywhere, the inherent will to enjoy, and the circumstantial will against enjoyment" (*T*, p. 310).

One of the essential features of "the circumstantial will against enjoyment," which only a few critics have considered, is Tess's own very powerful will against enjoyment.[3] It is almost unkind, it seems to some readers, to blame Tess—in any degree—for her misfortunes. A victim of sexual and spiritual violation, abandoned by her parents and the church, and the long-suffering plaything of the President of the Immortals, Tess is Hardy's most heartrending creation, his most unfairly abused heroine. But in pointing to Tess's self-destructiveness, we have no intention of attributing or even speaking of "blame." As Howe has said, the chastened, charitable Tess teaches such humility that we feel unqualified to judge her. Rather, as a critical judgment of a literary figure, it seems necessary—and fair—to describe Tess as an ambivalent woman in whose richly emotional nature impulses and imagination are at war with judgment; and it can be shown that Tess, by her choices, actions, and inaction, reveals her potent death instinct. Although the ultimate question for her is "To be, or not to be," her own character must be considered among her many victimizers.

In one tragic sense, she is "such an odd maid," as her mother calls her—the one in a thousand whose determination to enjoy cannot overcome the superhuman difficulties that oppose it. On the other hand, her self-defeating oddity is not so odd at all, as she is a child of the Durbeyfield household, whose "heads . . . chose to sail into difficulty, disaster, starvation, disease, degradation, death" (p. 49). She is a member of "a family harmless . . . to all except themselves" (p. 383), the daughter of a fatalistic mother and shiftless father, and it is no wonder that the much-victimized maid's behavior often contributes to her humiliation, her body's degradation, and finally her death.

If we examine Tess's actions in terms of their production of pleasure or pain, we notice disturbing patterns, as her choices and impulses are not directed toward or productive of enjoyment in life. This is shown in the very first scenes where she appears. At the May Day "club walking," when, traditionally, brides are chosen, Tess alone wears a red ribbon in her hair—suggesting her priority among celebrants of the local Cerealia—but Angel fails to observe her, "owing to her backwardness" in putting herself forward. With a look of reproach, Tess shows Angel her disappointment when he departs, and loses her "spirit to dance again for a long time, though she might have had plenty of partners" (p. 44). Later that night, when her parents are enjoying themselves at Mrs. Rolliver's, another "reproachful flash from Tess's dark eyes" brings the entertainment to an end. Later still, when her father is unable to deliver his beehives to Casterbridge, Tess rejects her mother's reasonable suggestion of asking one of the local men, "who were so much after dancing with 'ee yesterday," to make the delivery. Because Tess is too proud to seek a favor of an admirer, and too ashamed of her drunken father to let anyone know why he couldn't do his own work, she tries to drive the decrepit horse and wagon herself. On her darkling journey, Tess makes her famous judgment that our planet is a blighted

world. When the accident occurs in which the horse,
Prince, loses his life, Tess assumes full blame for her family's
misfortune, and the most telling aspects of the scene are
that Tess heaps reproach upon herself for her negligence
and regards herself "in the light of a murderess" for killing
Prince (p. 59). But the narrator makes it clear that "Nobody
blamed Tess as she blamed herself." Her immediate reaction
to the "oppressive sense of the harm she had done" leads
Tess to soften her resistance to her mother's scheme to
"claim kin" with the rich D'Urberville family. And this
scheme, of course, introduces her to Alec.

On this fatal day, then, we are given substantial insights
into Tess's character that help us understand the roots of her
self-destructiveness. Sometimes, in this tragedy of missed
opportunities, Tess's innocence and modesty, and sometimes her mistaken pride, prevent her from seizing the
promising occasion or securing her own best interest. Tess,
an inexperienced "vessel of emotion," is more sensitive to
her personal being and more conscientious about family and
business duties than her shiftless parents, and these distinctions give her a charm and spiritual superiority that are
lacking in her family. But it is this sensitivity and scru-
pulosity (products, perhaps, of her sixth-form level of
schooling) which reveal her subjection to collective social
influences that cut her off from her parents' customary and
healthily selfish pleasures, without which life cannot be
balanced.

That Tess should hold such a blighted view of existence is
not unusual, as Wessex country folk, of whom Joan Durbeyfield is a fair example, are inclined to a fatalistic view of
things. But Joan's fatalism is that of a happy child and is
tempered with the knowledge that "We must take the ups
wi' the downs"—and it doesn't keep her out of the pub or
prevent her from seizing life's main chances when they

present themselves. We can imagine, for example, with what delight she played her trump card when she was of courting age! And her fatalistic attributions of blame—to God or nature—insulate her from guilt and preserve her from worrying about repairing evils that an external power caused. In contrast, Tess's dark views seem to have sunk deeper into her nature, where they are not easily countered by the usual pleasures of life. Clearly, in one who lacks Joan's resilience—and especially in a young, sensitive, healthy, and beautiful girl—such gloomy thoughts about existence are portents of a painful future.

What is truly disturbing, however, is Tess's handling of her guilt after Prince's death. Hardy seems to have understood (with Freud) that the sense of guilt is an expression of ambivalence; in particular, it reveals the eternal struggle between Eros and the instinct of destruction. Now Tess's self-accusation as a murderess is extravagantly impulsive. Not only the blaming, however, but her repeated heaping of reproach upon herself reveal the intensity of Tess's self-destructiveness: they amount to a subversive denigration of her worth as a person. There is something positively morbid in Tess's response—and nothing that could even remotely be viewed as life affirming.

This radical inability to manage guilt overburdens Tess's conscience and leads her to exaggerate her responsibility to retrieve her family's fortunes. Thus her resistance to Joan's scheme for calling on Mrs. D'Urberville is ineffective, and she permits herself to be "put . . . in the way of a grand marriage," even though her judgment can find but "doubtful profit" in the enterprise. At Mrs. Rolliver's, when Joan and Jack first discuss the plan, Jack is wary about his daughter's willingness; both are well aware of Tess's recalcitrance, her tendency to reject what is likely to benefit her. "Tess is queer," is Jack's way of explaining his daughter's behavior.

But Joan is confident of having her way, as she replies: "But she's tractable at bottom. Leave her to me" (p. 52).

When, finally, Joan sends her daughter away, Tess has been able to allay, though not dispel, her ominous feelings about her new position. Like a victim accepting her sacrificial fate, Tess permits her mother's every wish "with calm abandonment," and Joan washes her, dresses her in the white frock of May Day, and prepares her child to appear as a woman ready for the altar. The full intent of all these preparations must be masked, however, in fear that Tess would rebel if too much were made of Alec's fancy for her and her good chance. "She is such an odd maid that it mid zet her against him, or against going there, even now." But Tess puts herself completely in her mother's hands: "Do what you like with me, mother"; and Joan "was only too delighted at this tractability" (p. 74).

It is precisely this tractability, this inability to resist external pressure when her judgment is overpowered by guilt, that Tess carries to The Slopes and Alec D'Urberville. At her first meeting with Alec, Tess is both attracted to and repelled by him, but unable to resist his demands. He can make her blush with his flattery and can distress her with his pressing manner; and when he insists that she accompany him, Tess, despite her wishes, consents. When he forces her to eat strawberries from his hand, in a moment that foreshadows the seduction in the Chase, she again obeys, submitting—here, as she will there, — "like one in a dream," and she continues "eating in a half-pleased, half-reluctant state whatever d'Urberville offers her" (p. 66). If her mother has dressed her for sacrifice, Alec accepts the offering and bedecks her with flowers of passion, but Tess's ambivalent feelings make her unconscious of the various ill omens which we perceive, so that only the rose thorn that pricks her chin seems ominous to Tess. "Thus the thing began," and though, for now, Alec resists kissing the tempting woman-child, he has learned—as Joan knows—that "she's tractable at bottom."

The pattern for their relationship is established at this first meeting. In submitting to her mother's scheme, Tess is required to submit to Alec's advances; and on their second meeting, after she is forced to hold onto his waist, her submission is symbolized when she receives "the kiss of mastery." Tess, clearly, underestimates her danger, as Alec's attentions are not obnoxious. Instead of childishly vacillating, she decides against returning home and abandoning the scheme for rehabilitation of her family. Thus she pursues the position she undertook in guilt, under the careful cultivation of Alec's flattering attentions.

The seduction in The Chase, to which Tess is subjected after "abandoning herself to her impulse" to triumph over Car Darch, is one of the most controversial scenes in Hardy—not only because of ambiguity about what happens in the darkness and silence of The Chase, but also because of Tess's ambivalent feelings about Alec. Thus, while her behavior is innocent and, with Car, self-affirming, Tess is not without responsibility for her misfortune, for she is inclined to abandon herself, both to her mother's scheme and to her present impulse, at precisely those moments when she should be most careful.

An essential insight about the dangers of impulse is presented in the novel's opening scene, where Parson Tringham recounts to Jack Durbeyfield the "useless piece of information" about his ancestry. The parson's antiquarian enthusiasm overcame his resolve not to disturb Jack with the curious and profitless bit of lore: "However, our impulses are too strong for our judgment sometimes" (p. 33). This apparently trivial indiscretion adumbrates one of the novel's decisive perceptions, and its consequence is to propel Tess upon her tragic course, just as in *Far from the Madding Crowd* Bathsheba's frivolous impulse to send Boldwood a valentine—another apparently insignificant act—is sufficient to initiate his self-destruction. What Hardy suggests, with both the parson's and Tess's impulses, is far from trivial. It is as ancient as Plato, as modern as Matthew Arnold: a person can unleash destructive forces when his impulses are not in harmony with his judgment. Continually evident in this novel is the damaging effect of self-division, and nowhere is this clearer than when Tess's untimely impulse delivers her from Car Darch into the far more threatening company of Alec.

While Hardy relies on subtle and indirect techniques for building ambiguity, the scene in The Chase reveals how Tess's judgment is blurred because of her emotional confusion over Alec. Though she admits she doesn't love him, and believes she cannot help herself at The Slopes, she has remained there for three months, during which Alec repeatedly made her angry. But Alec knows that her feelings toward him are not frigid. In fact, her refusal to reply to his questions tells him—and us—more about her emotions than perhaps she herself knows. Tess will not admit that she feels obliged to Alec for rescuing her from the Amazonian Darch, because her sense of obligation cannot dispel the dubiousness of her situation. Had she not felt obliged to him, we should have expected her to say so, as she has never before missed an opportunity to tell Alec the offensive truth.

On the other hand, she cannot lie to him when he asks if she has always been offended by his lovemaking; nor can she trust the truth to pass her lips, now that she is alone with him in the forest. When he rails at her for trifling with his feelings and eluding him, and wants to treat her as a lover and clasp her in his arms, Tess is unsure of how to respond. "I don't know—I wish—how can I say yes or no when—," she answers; but when he clasps her, as he desires, "Tess expressed no further negative" (p. 98). When they get lost in the woods, Tess is both arch and truly dismayed at his treachery. When Alec tells of his gifts to her family, she is both grateful and pained. As Alec leaves her, Tess falls into the passivity of reverie, distressed by the sudden vision of his passion for her and his generosity to her family, as she considers it. Soon, sleep overtakes her, relieving her temporarily of her oppressive thoughts and ambivalent emotions.

This whole complex of her feelings and the scene's symbolical suggestiveness creates the ambiguous context of Tess's seduction. However, there is an unavoidable implication of self-sacrifice in Tess's violation by Alec, after she abandoned herself to sleep (which traditionally is considered "death's second self" and a symbol of man's retreat from or evasion of personal responsibility). Nevertheless, the ambiguity of the scene is inevitable, for Hardy understood Tess's "natural" need and desire to express affection and gratitude to Alec, in spite of her "cultivated" inhibitions. Like Maggie Tulliver in George Eliot's *Mill on the Floss*, Tess could not "decide" to give herself—could not, that is, give rational assent to Alec's lovemaking; and she could not, with her overly civilized conscience, go through the act pleasurably and without tears. But in Hardy's brilliant discovery of a technique for registering her complex psychological state, Tess drifts into sleep as Maggie drifts down the river. When she is "taken" by Alec, her physical exhaustion and mental quandary permit a decision that she can neither condone nor evade.

Tess's subsequent account of their relationship confirms her ambivalence with Alec: she insists she had never sincerely loved him, but "My eyes were dazed by you for a little, and that was all" (p. 105). And after Tess returns home and replies to the local girls' inquiries about the legendary heartbreaker, she experiences moments of superiority and, "in spite of thought," recognizes that her "experiences in the field of courtship had, indeed, been slightly enviable" (pp. 112 – 13). Nevertheless, the result of her self-division is her transformation, at a single stroke, into "another girl than the simple one she had been at home," and the nature of her change is figured by Hardy's descriptions of her movements: she rests on a gate "in a mechanical way," sits and replies to Alec "like a puppet," and receives his masterful kiss, which recalls the first one he gave her, "like a marble term." Still, despite these suggestions of the reduction or diminution of Tess's humanity, she will not become Alec's "creature" by taking things from a man she doesn't love. This remnant of honor is the only positive feeling she registers in the tawdry departure scene.

Again, Tess's sense of guilt so overpowers her that she is her worst accuser. Although the narrator sympathizes with her for her misfortune, and readers share that sympathy, and even feel admiration for her, she speaks of loathing and hating herself for her weakness. Even Alec tries to shake her out of her absurd melancholy, as he calls it; yet the depth of her feeling is registered in her wish that she had never been born. Now the distance between this wish and a desire for death is very short, and if there is a leitmotif in Tess's life henceforth, it is reiteration of her hope to be in her grave. We see her back in her father's house, feeling terrible depression and wanting to hide herself in a tomb (p. 113), and we watch her nurse her baby in the fields, wishing she and the child were in the churchyard (p. 118). Hardy describes Tess's "quiescent glide" in terms of her guilty conscience and oppressive imagination:

> At times her whimsical fancy would intensify natural processes around her till they seemed a part of her own story. Rather they

> became a part of it; for the world is only a psychological phe-
> nomenon, and what they seemed they were. The midnight airs
> and gusts, moaning amongst the tightly-wrapped buds and bark
> of the winter twigs, were formulae of bitter reproach. [p. 114]

Because she associates herself with Aholah and Aholibah
(the two prostitutes in Ezekiel 23:2–35) and because she
has shared Job's loathing of life and his choice of strangling
and death, Tess perversely opposes her vital nature by
trying to lead a repressed life. For this commitment, the
result of her perverse imagination, Tess will ultimately succumb. As the narrator makes perfectly clear, Tess's sense of
herself "as a figure of Guilt intruding into the haunts of
Innocence" is "a sorry and mistaken creation of Tess's
fancy—a cloud of moral hobgoblins by which she was ter-
rified without reason" (p. 114).[4]

Tess's life, however, does not move directly to destruction, as the battle between the death instinct and her
powerful vitality must take its full course, and in the next
phase, with resurgence of the tendency to find sweet pleasure somewhere, Tess embarks on her marvelous rally. Under the urgings of the pulse of hopeful life, she tries to
escape the past and obliterate her consciousness of her
failed effort to claim kin with the D'Urbervilles. "Was once
lost always lost really true of chastity? she would ask herself.
She might prove it false if she could veil bygones. The
recuperative power which pervaded organic nature was
surely not denied to maidenhood alone" (p. 127).

Her resolution upon departing shows the firm judgment
of the complex woman she has become since her "liberal
education" (as the narrator terms it). "On one point she was
resolved: there should be no more d'Urberville air-castles in
the dreams and deeds of her new life. She would be the
dairymaid Tess, and nothing more" (pp. 127–28). Unfortunately, she is as incapable of being just a dairymaid as Jude

is of being simply a stone mason; and for all the wisdom of such a resolve, it is simply impossible for one with her emotional nature and intellectual potential to achieve.

Ironically the subjective imagination that causes Tess so much suffering is an important element in her renewal at Talbothays. Like her mother, who possessed the dubious wisdom of shutting her eyes to Jack's defects of character and regarding him only as the ideal lover, Tess tends at first to see Angel as more than a man. And though he is most often criticized for his depersonalizing idealization of Tess (she is "a visionary essence of woman—a whole sex condensed into one typical form"), she succumbs to that nearly universal impulse of lovers. Tess seems to regard him "as an intelligence rather than as a man," whose mental attitude quite dejected and disheartened her (p. 153).

The dangers of Tess's idealization of Angel are suggested by the narrator, who provides a corrective view to Tess's by insisting how "absurdly far" Angel is from the disinterested, chivalrous, protective lover he seems to her. Still, though she loves him, her sense of his vast superiority leads Tess to the "self-immolation" of encouraging him to choose one of the other milkmaids for his wife. Eventually, though, Angel's persistence overcomes her religious determination never to be tempted to marry again, and the gradual development of their relationship—particularly the triumph of Tess's loving nature over her self-repressive scrupulousness—is one of the finest portrayals in all of Hardy's novels. The "appetite for joy" is clearly ascendant, for Angel "was so godlike in her eyes" (p. 210) that her affection for him is the breath and life of her being.[5]

It is characteristic of Tess, however, to jeopardize her happiness with Angel as soon as she consents to marry him.

Her impulse to tell him her history flies directly in the face
of her mother's advice not to trumpet her "bygone trouble."
Her "childish nature," which compels her to tell all,
exasperates Joan. Unconsciously, it seems, the "odd maid"
is determined to suffer still. But the letter containing her
confession miscarries, and Tess soon finds herself married to
the man who seemed immortal to her, the man she idolized.

Throughout her wedding day, Tess is besieged by feelings
of guilt and unworthiness, and could not know how soon she
would realize her chief wish, expressed when she was dressing earlier in the day. "Her one desire, so long resisted, to
make herself his, to call him her lord, her own—then, if
necessary, to die" (p. 239), is a compound of her intensely
idolatrous love with her profound guilt-ridden fatality. The
desire to die, so evident before the rally, resurfaces on her
wedding night, when Tess's good fortune exacerbates her
sense of guilt and renews her conscience's demand for
punishment. The form her mortification will take is suggested by her reaction to Retty's attempted suicide. (This
response, furthermore, is the key to the meaning of her life
after marriage.) Tess is depressed by Retty's action, but
when Angel tells her that the maid was naturally morbid,
Tess claims she had no cause to be, "While they who have
cause to be, hide it, and pretend they are not."

> This incident . . . turned the scale for her. They [the dairymaids
> Izz, Marian, Retty] were simple and innocent girls on whom the
> unhappiness of unrequited love had fallen; they had deserved
> better at the hands of Fate. She had deserved worse—yet she was
> the chosen one. It was wicked of her to take all without paying.
> She would pay to the uttermost farthing. [p. 250]

In her sympathy for the girls, Tess seems to forget her
own suffering and that she, too, may have deserved a better
fate. But her guilt at concealing her weakness with Alec—a

chance misfortune that she regarded with the rigorousness of conventional morality—convinces her that she doesn't deserve her good fortune, and calls for punishment. The perversity of this moral scorekeeping is manifest in her determination to pay, and the confession at Wellbridge Manor, a first installment of her self-inflicted penance, commences Tess's martyrdom. Unlike the ascetic Giles, the type of martyr who submits to the unpleasant or the intolerable out of devotion to his ideal, Tess is the kind who causes herself to be the victim of cruelty at the hands of circumstances or another person.[6] Knowing that Tess intends to make herself pay to the "uttermost farthing" for her wickedness, we see that her subsequent behavior has all the coherence of a martyr's. What she proposes in this scene, she devotes the rest of her life to achieving.

One of the easiest decisions that Tess ever makes is to forgive Angel for his "eight-and-forty hours' dissipation with a stranger" because Angel, her very human and limited lover, is the object of her idolatry: the god before whom she places her guilt and to whose judgment and punishment she willingly submits. More insidiously, her devotion to him as an infinitely superior being not only rules out her condemning him, it also reinforces her sense of unworthiness and her tendency toward self-pity and self-sacrifice. Tess's real terror is apparent as soon as she has made Angel see her as she sees herself: "a guilty woman in the guise of an innocent one." Being "deadened" by his view of her and reduced to "a flood of self-sympathetic tears" seem only natural, as she never wavers in her need to love and be loved by him. It is simply that her other need, to immolate herself, which operates on a deeper level of her consciousness, is on the ascendant. This is startlingly eloquent when, literally minutes after her confession, Tess suggests that she does not belong to Angel and refuses to ask him to let her live with him "because [she has] no right to!" She promises not to follow him if he leaves her; not to ask why, if he never speaks to her anymore; and to "obey you like your wretched slave, even if it is to lie down and die" (p. 256).

Later that night, throughout the brief honeymoon, and until she dies, Tess continues to pay. Patterns of behavior, first operant in the confession scene, recur until Tess's will to live is overcome and she despairs of Angel's returning to her. Henceforth Tess will act to achieve her explicit intentions: "to let him for whom she lived and breathed despise her if he would" and to make her mother regard her as a fool (p. 228).

In her shock and distress, Tess provokes Angel's antagonism and reproach by pleading "things that would have been better left to silence." Conversely, when Angel's soul might be moved, she fails to touch the "back current of sympathy" in him because "she took everything as her deserts, and hardly opened her mouth." In this instance, as in many later ones, Tess does the thing that injures her and fails to do what might retrieve Angel's heart. That she has not the arts of a woman of the world, that she knows not the power of weeping and hysterics for conquering her lover's fastidiousness, are indicative of her powerlessness to avoid the fate she has chosen. Another way of putting it is to say that Tess is not made to survive.

In her perceptive remarks on Tess's behavior in similar circumstances, Evelyn Hardy points out that passivity and inaction can sometimes be as destructive as action.[7] Thus, whether it is her "pitiful" devotion to Angel, her sense that she has no right to tamper with his life, her refusal to "anger him, grieve him, stultify him," or her "mood of long-suffering" (on no fewer than four occasions *before* he leaves her),

Tess "made his way easy for him, and she herself was his best advocate."[8] The narrator implies that Angel could not have withstood Tess's pleading, and regrets that "the many effective chords which she could have stirred by an appeal were left untouched." Thus Tess submits to Angel's departure "because you know best what my punishment ought to be" (p. 278).

Because Tess persists in considering Angel her lord, she must endure humiliation, deprivation, and further sexual abuse. She cannot return to her father's home, as she has caused her mother to regard her as "a little fool" (p. 281), and she is forced to seek hard work at a "starve-acre place" to support herself. Moreover, Tess repeatedly fails to take advantage of her position as Angel's wife, notably when it means warding off poverty and her physically exhausting, spiritually demeaning existence at Flintcomb-Ash. Even the few pounds he left her are "consecrated" souvenirs. The narrator rebukes Tess for the "delicacy, pride, false shame, whatever it may be called, on Clare's account," which hindered her from claiming from her in-laws "the fair allowance he had left her." (The phrase "whatever it may be called" implies that the narrator, her most sympathetic advocate, is exasperated by Tess's indefinable perversity in denying herself what is rightly hers.) Tess's reply to Marian, who is shocked by the unfairness of a gentleman's wife's working in the swedes and cornfields, shows the martyr's fidelity to her tyrannical god: "O yes it is, quite fair; though I am very unhappy." Under no circumstance will Tess bring reproach upon Angel's name or treatment of her. To her conscience, that she should be punished by him is "quite fair" (p. 307).

Tess's commitment to Angel requires her fiercest loyalty, for the longer he makes her suffer, the harder she must strain to sustain her love. She must repel all casual lovers, such as the young men at Chalk-Newton. Tess claims she

hates "all other men, and [likes] to make 'em think scorn-
fully of me!" There is something akin to self-mutilation in
her efforts to preserve herself from "aggressive admiration,"
for the good looks that have caused so much trouble are
effaced. Tess puts on her oldest, least attractive fieldgown
and wraps her face in a handkerchief to hide her features;
then she "mercilessly nipped her eyebrows off" (p. 304). All
this is done to preserve her good looks for Angel, from
whom she still hopes to hear compliments! Could the ambivalence of her motives and the struggle between her life
and death instincts be more touchingly rendered than in
Tess's paradoxical destroying-in-order-to-preserve?

Unfortunately, Alec appears and renews his importunities
before Tess hears from Angel. Her faith in her husband
received a severe setback when she learned of Angel's proposal to take Izz with him to Brazil, and the brutality of her
work is eroding her vitality. It is in this dispiriting context
that her tormentor confronts her. The vehemence of her
self-destructive impulse is evident when Alec taunts Tess by
accusing her for his backsliding and tells her to "leave that
mule you call your husband for ever." Instinctively, she
strikes him and draws blood; then tells him: "'Now, punish
me!' . . .'Whip me, crush me; . . . I shall not cry out. Once
victim, always victim—that's the law'" (p. 354).

Tess's will to live is wearing thin; her determination to die
is gaining force. Whereas she previously asked, "Was once
lost always lost really true of chastity?" she now eagerly
imagines—as insuperable—a savage law that serves her unconscious interest. The world which Hardy described earlier, as enlivened by the invincible instinct toward self-
delight and moved by the tremendous force of the "appetite
for joy," has not changed; and Tess's perception of it, for all
its poignant sincerity, sounds painfully subjective. Like the
young men at Chalk-Newton and her employer at Flint-

comb-Ash, Alec attacks Tess in lust for her body, which she values only because it belongs to Angel. As she writes in her frantic appeal to him, her looks may be the "one thing about me worth your having" (p. 360). When Tess repulses Alec and calls out for punishment, her hopeless defiance gives the cry its tragic ring.

Tess's one desire—to love Angel, then die—has directed her life since she consented to marry him. She has called him "lord" and tried to make herself his, even though both have thought she is Alec's wife in nature.[9] But her idolatry of the man, her delight in loving him, have led her to the violent end she anticipated and effected. Though she proclaimed to Angel on her wedding night that "I love you for ever—in all changes, in all disgraces, because you are yourself" (p. 255), Tess is as capable as he of being in love with an illusion. The Angel she loved never existed—or, put another way, the man she loved ceased to exist after Tess's confession, and the man she continues to love is not "her" Angel. When Tess is finally disillusioned and realizes how monstrously Angel has treated her, how cruel and unjust he has been, she feels she can never forgive him and tries to forget him.[10] Her faith in Angel is destroyed when Tess is near despair over her homeless family and Alec again presses her to become his "creature." She can resist dependence on Alec if she asks for money from her father-in-law, but Alec retorts: "*If* you ask for it. But you won't, Tess; I know you, you'll never ask for it—you'll starve first!" (p. 379). No one— not even Joan Durbeyfield—knows the "odd maid" as thoroughly as Alec.

Alienation from Angel leaves Tess spiritually dead—as though her god has died or, more appropriately, abandoned her. Since her "murder" of Prince, her "fall" to Alec, and her "sin" in marrying Angel, Tess has accumulated so much irreparable guilt and self-loathing that her life has long been worthless to her. Only as long as she believed she had some value for Angel, if only in her good looks, has she resisted the impulse to end her life. When, in the sleep-walking scene, it seemed so fit, so desirable, to be dashed to pieces with Angel, Tess rejected the impulse to secure the luxury of death—just as, twice earlier on the same night, she rejected killing herself in consideration for Angel's reputation (pp. 250, 265). Her rationalization of her suicidal wishes reveals what Evelyn Hardy has called her "insidious need to immolate herself under the deceptive guise of benefiting others."[11] Clare has tried to convince Tess of how unworthy these self-destructive wishes are.

> "But, Angel," [Tess] pleaded, enlarging her eyes in calm unconcern upon him, "it was thought of entirely on your account—to set you free without the scandal of the divorce that I thought you would have to get. I should never have dreamt of doing it on mine. However, to do it with my own hand is too good for me, after all. It is you, my ruined husband, who ought to strike the blow. I think I should love you more, if that were possible, if you could bring yourself to do it, since there's no other way of escape for 'ee. I feel I am so utterly worthless! So very greatly in the way!" [p. 265]

And she acquiesces—believing, no doubt, that she has no wish opposed to his. The intensity of her masochistic impulse to martyr herself is equalled only by Sue Bridehead in *Jude the Obscure*.

The form of Tess's self-destruction is foreshadowed at the plantation outside Chalk-Newton, where Tess feels the eye sockets under her skin and thinks of the time when "that bone would be bare. 'I wish it were now,' she said" (p. 301). Her flesh, which has caused her so much misery and which she thinks no longer seems desirable even to Angel, shall bear the sting of her self-flagellation. That this is her intention is symbolically indicated when she breaks the necks of the wounded pheasants to put them out of their misery. A wounded bird herself, so to speak, convinced that life is worse than vanity, she will soon place herself beyond suffering with her weaker fellows in nature's teeming family.

Once she despairs of Angel's returning to her, Tess's spirit is virtually destroyed—her subsequent existence a mere death-in-life until her physical vitality atrophies or is similarly destroyed. When Tess returns to Alec and trades her flesh for his maintenance of her and her family, she becomes a creature who has spiritually ceased to recognize her body, "allowing it to drift, like a corpse upon the current, in a direction dissociated from its living will" (p. 401).

On his wedding night, Angel seemed to detect a sinister design in the countenance of the d'Urberville dame whose portrait hung over the entrance to Tess's bedchamber. He sensed "a concentrated purpose of revenge on the other sex" in the face that so resembled Tess's. This remarkable impression is followed by another which, though the narrator casts doubt on its validity, may be truer than the narrator—or Hardy, for that matter—realizes. Angel wonders if Tess's "eyes which as they gazed never expressed any divergence from what the tongue was telling, were yet ever seeing another world behind her ostensible one, discordant and contrasting" (p. 261).

Tess's eyes and tongue seem to represent the conflict between her unconscious and conscious motives, her internal division, which neither Angel nor the narrator has the vocabulary to describe but which both are acute enough to sense. Can it be, then, that Tess enacts her inherited vengeance against men when she returns to Alec—that her joining him symbolizes both her own depersonalization and her righteous sexual reaction against Angel for rejecting her as his wife? In angry words, Tess tells Angel that Alec "has won me back again" (p. 401), as though her body were the prize in a contest between them.

And is not Angel's second impression his awareness of the very ambivalence in Tess that long prevented her from consenting to become his wife, and which she utters before, finally, she capitulates to Alec: "Never in her life—she could swear it from the bottom of her soul—had she ever intended to do wrong. . . . Whatever her sins, they were not sins of intention, but of inadvertence"? (p. 379). We must agree that she has not consciously intended to sin against Angel, but her impluse to destroy herself—even though she sublimates her self-destructiveness by martyring herself to Angel—is expressed so often in her conscious words and subconscious impulses and acts that it cannot be denied. It is possible that the violence she inherits from her d'Urberville ancestors is employed in the service of her own self-destructive intention.

Angel's return to reclaim his abandoned wife restores Tess's fidelity to her idol and exacerbates her guilt for having been unfaithful to him, and her anger against Angel is displaced upon Alec for leading her away and destroying her chances for happiness. It is not in madness that she kills Alec, but in plausible outrage. Her complex motivation includes, perhaps, a modicum of unconscious frustration for her inability to avenge herself against Angel; and this combination of violent emotions turns her into a murderess.

The fury of Tess's anger, despair, and sexual revenge claims Alec as its first victim, but in becoming a murderess, Tess puts herself under the psychological "law of talion," which demands the life of the killer. Thus Tess herself is the second victim of her desperate rage against the man who has torn her life to pieces; and her accumulated guilt is too heavy to be borne any longer. By committing a capital crime and making herself subject to hanging, Tess is as much a suicide as Farmer Boldwood—as self-destructive as if she had turned the bloody knife upon herself. Tess not only realizes this, but welcomes her long-delayed death. She knows that "What must come will come" in a few weeks.

Though she had once determined to make Angel despise her, in the New Forest, on their flight from Sandbourne, Tess is resolute in not wanting to outlive his present feeling for her: "I would rather be dead and buried when the time comes for you to despise me, so that it may never be known to me that you despised me" (p. 413). Moreover, with the recurrence of youthful belief, Tess proceeds to her altruistic sacrifice in the hope that she and Angel will meet again after death. Like the martyr she has been since she loved Angel, she views death as the means of reunion with a beloved deity after expiation for her sins.[12] Angel does not destroy that hope. When the authorities come for her, Tess murmurs: "It is as it should be. . . . Angel, I am almost glad— yes, glad! This happiness could not have lasted. It was too much. I have had enough; and now I shall not live for you to despise me!" Finally, on an altar of Stonehenge and on a gibbet in Wintoncester, Tess's self-destructive life reaches "fulfilment."

Rarely has the President of the Immortals found so willing a victim to share in his sport.

CHAPTER TEN

"I'd Have My Life Unbe"

THE COMMENT IN *Jude the Obscure* about the "coming universal wish not to live" can hardly be deemed an unconsidered prophecy, a fantastic specter raised by Hardy's taking too seriously his creation of the unnaturally gloomy Little Father Time. Rather, as I have tried to demonstrate throughout this study, the context for considering that disturbing phrase must include Hardy's long-evolving sensitivity to modern man's declining zest for life and his conviction that thought was robbing existence of its joyousness and making life a heavy burden. Hardy's narrator goes so far as to predict that in future years there will be *more* Judes and Sues, who "will see weltering humanity still more vividly than [they] do now . . . and will be afraid to reproduce" (p. 299).

It is possible to argue that Sue greatly exaggerated when she reasons that "Everybody is getting to feel as [we] do" and that in fifty, a hundred years, their feelings will be commonplace. Some may feel that it is unthinkable for anyone but a deranged masochist, or her pessimistic creator, to imagine the human race putting an end to itself by its refusal to reproduce. But this idea is not uniquely Sue's, nor an exclusively literary notion. The speaker in "I Said to Love" utters the very same sentiment (*CP*, #77), while innumerable young couples in the contemporary Western world, though they may not think of ending the human race, recoil before images of "weltering humanity" and have—for fear of war, poverty, malnutrition, etc. —either "limited" their families or refused to begin them. Hardy has even suggested that the human race would be wiser to annihilate itself rather than continue to exalt war.[1]

If such prophecies and admonishments seem too audacious, we must not forget that Hardy's imagination was frighteningly courageous in searching the dark passages that modern man was charting for himself. Nor was he less courageous in uttering the startling, terrifying impressions he formed as a result of his immersion in the destructive element of modern life. Such speculations suggest that Hardy had given deep thought to the rationality of suicide in the Godless, absurd modern world, to the inexorable logicality of self-destruction for increasing numbers who are unaided by the "imperishable truths" which alone, Wordsworth says in "Tintern Abbey," "can utterly abolish or destroy . . . all that is at enmity with joy." Was he not simply exploring the modern situation that Ivan Karamazov defined when he said that, without belief in God and immortality, everything would be possible?

Perhaps the shock of Hardy's sentiments is reduced if we recall that such respectable Victorians as Alfred Tennyson and Charles Kingsley, in 1872 and 1850, expressed attitudes that are very close to Hardy's when they considered the worth of life without the "imperishable truths." Discussing immortality, Tennyson stated: "If I ceased to believe in any chance of another life, and of a great Personality somewhere in the Universe, I should not care a pin for anything." And the robust Kingsley declared that if God were a deceiver, "I'd go and blow my brains out and be rid of the whole thing at once, I would indeed."[2]

There are in the novels other, less startling impressions about the reasonableness of suicide. Gabriel Oak, a most sensible and morally reliable man, implies that suicide is not always the act of a deranged, unreasonable person, for he refused to accept a jury's verdict that Boldwood was insane when he killed Troy. Also, Clym Yeobright is contrasted with young men in France who commit suicide when they realize "the grimness of the general human situation," but in England, Hardy's narrator tells us, a young man does better or (and here is the telling implication) much worse by remaining alive (*RN*, p. 205).

It seems to me that Hardy was too deeply versed in the Old Testament, too familiar with classical drama and ancient philosophy, too spiritually akin to the great Romantic artists in their understanding of the death instinct and the paradoxical proximity of love and death, *not* to have considered suicide a reasonable option for some people. Moreoever, its "reasonableness" increases as man's estrangement from God and his fellow man deepens, his capacity for joy atrophies, and his opportunities for experiencing pleasure and love decrease.

A measure of the accuracy of Hardy's prophetic impression about the "coming universal wish not to live" may be that, after his death, many more people were speaking and thinking seriously about suicide. Albert Camus, in *The Myth of Sisyphus*, wrote some fifty years after Hardy's career as a novelist ended: "There is but one truly philosophical problem, and that is suicide." And there is Morse Peckham's comment, about seventy-five years after *Jude:*

> All of us spend a certain amount of time longing for death. We are
> all half in love with it, for to love is to interpret a real or potential

stimulus as offering the reduction of all tension, and death is necessarily imagined as a stimulus. Suicide, then, is a rational act, invariably based upon the values of the belief-system, invariably justified by cultural metaphysics. After all, some cultures approve of it most heartily, perhaps with wisdom. No, it is not suicide that is irrational, but the determination to live, in spite of all reasons to the contrary.[3]

Popular attention to the "coming universal wish not to live" has been focused by the suicide in recent years of innumerable public figures, including the literary artists Hemingway, Berryman, Mishima, Plath, Sexton, and by the startling statistics which reveal suicide to be, apart from accidents, the leading cause of death among Americans in the 15–24 age group ("dropping out," drug addiction, and alcoholism among the young are indirect or "chronic" forms of self-destruction, social scientists tell us).

This reality, as well as the extraordinarily high suicide rate in Sweden, a nation considered extremely fortunate in many ways, continues to baffle the common man. Increasingly, however, such realities are getting his attention. The horror of the Jonestown mass suicide may be perceived as an outburst of madness; but the very existence of Jonestown, and other communities like it, represents total repudiation of the "normal" modes of modern existence. Observers of contemporary events have indirectly attested to the pervasiveness of modern man's disenchantment with his transient, urban, spiritless existence. Such phrases as "suicidal excesses" or "self-destructive tendencies" are often used in commentaries on (for example) the race riots of the 1960s, America's isolationist instincts after Vietnam, legislative paroxysms following Watergate, and, most recently, Iran's rejection of "progress" and its commitment to "martyrdom" rather than "westernization." Everywhere, as modern life becomes more intolerable, more people are choosing not to tolerate life.

It is no longer necessary, it seems to me, to debate whether Hardy was serious about the "coming universal wish not to live." Now it is time to try to understand his vision of self-destructiveness as it functions within his novels. Hardy's impressions and perceptions, I submit, are neither excessively morbid, idiosyncratic, nor intrinsically shocking. Rather, they evolve as a logical elaboration of views, available to and sometimes explicitly articulated in the works of his Victorian contemporaries, who had not fully penetrated—or fearfully backed off from representing—the human consequences of honestly living out the modernist premises.[4]

The depth of Hardy's prophetic gloom is apparent, however, if we consider that the "interfusing effect of poetry" and his tenuous ideal of "loving-kindness" alone stand in the way of the world's perishing. His books, he once said, represent an extended indictment of man's inhumanity to man. Yet unlike Wordsworth, who also deplored what man has made of man, Hardy rarely permits us to put aside the burden of the painful mysteries, rarely makes us feel the joy of living. He is, indisputably, a great seer, though not a soaring singer like Shelley's skylark. He may be described, in his own words, as a "bird deprived of wings," who nevertheless cries to us, through his pain, to be charitable.

Any alliance between religion and complete rationality, he says, may be "a forlorn hope, a mere dream";[5] but Hardy never gives up on love. That the suffering of men can be relieved if they will love one another—that the agonies of Eustacia, Giles, Tess, and Jude might have been reduced through loving-kindness—is the gleam that brightens even his bleakest, apparently most negative fictions. Herein, it seems to me, is the key to Hardy's artistic uses of adversity: through the self-destruction of his characters, he asserts life's fragile preciousness most dramatically. Suffering and suicide are transmuted in his works to enforce a saving sympathy.

In his diagnosis of his culture's maladies, Hardy searches the human heart of darkness that our eyes are too weak or reluctant to probe, and his "obstinate questionings" and "blank misgivings" are often deeply disturbing. Yet, with Matthew Arnold, Hardy is one of the "saving remnant"; and even in the frightening murk of human self-destructiveness, his eyes strained to see the "way to the Better." His courageous sincerity permitted, even required, Hardy to portray man's vulnerability to self-destruction. But, as do all the greatest artists, Hardy teaches us not only that we must die (often by our own hand); he passionately reminds us how to live.

Notes

PREFACE

1. See Bailey's "Evolutionary Meliorism in the Poetry of Thomas Hardy," *Studies in Philology*, 60 (July 1963): 569, and his *Thomas Hardy and the Cosmic Mind* (Chapel Hill: University of North Carolina Press, 1956), p. 160.

2. Robert Gittings, *Young Thomas Hardy* (London: Heinemann, 1975), p. 186. Subsequent references to this work will be cited *YH*.

CHAPTER ONE

1. F. E. Hardy, *The Life of Thomas Hardy* (London: Macmillan, 1962), p. 153. Subsequent references to this work will be cited *L*.

2. See *Thomas Hardy's Personal Writings*, ed. Harold Orel (Lawrence: University of Kansas Press, 1966), p. 39. Subsequent references to this work will be cited *PW*.

3. But see Dale Kramer, *Thomas Hardy: The Forms of Tragedy* (Detroit: Wayne State University Press, 1975), with whose readings of *The Woodlanders* and *Tess* I disagree.

4. Gittings, *YH*, p. 35.

5. Albert J. Guerard, *Thomas Hardy* (Cambridge, Mass.: Harvard University Press, 1949), p. 37.

6. See David J. DeLaura, "'The Ache of Modernism' in Hardy's Later Novels," *Journal of English Literary History,* 34 (1967): 396, 399.

7. See Gittings, *YH,* p. 5, on the prose style of the *Life:* Hardy's "idea of narrative had degenerated into a set of clumsily-connected anecdotes, often, it seems, chosen for quaintness or oddity rather than for relevance to the main themes of his life." But Gittings' insight about Hardy's reaction to the hanging of James Seale reveals—what seems to me—the book's essential value: "Hardy is disturbed not by the event nor the moral and social ideas connected with it, but by his own sensations at the moment, and his own isolation" (p. 35). This is precisely the kind of revelation that opens inroads to the author's idiosyncrasy. Few writers, I hardly need add, have traveled as attentively and assiduously as Dr. Gittings over the main roads and byways of Hardy's life.

8. Gittings' treatment of Moule's influence on Hardy should be read in its entirety (pp. 37–42 and 178–86 in *YH*).

9. Michael Millgate, *Thomas Hardy: His Career as a Novelist* (New York: Random House, 1971), pp. 237–43.

10. But see Millgate, p. 239, for his discussion of the suicide of M. Quinn as a prototype of Abel in *The Mayor of Casterbridge.*

11. See *L,* pp. 278–79. Also see *PW,* p. 129, where Hardy argues the necessity of "the crash of broken commandments" for bringing about tragedy.

12. Michael Millgate, *Thomas Hardy: A Biography* (New York: Random House, 1982), p. 16.

13. See James Gibson's edition of *The Complete Poems of Thomas Hardy* (London: Macmillan, 1976), #492. Subsequent references to this edition will be cited *CP.*

14. See Robert Gittings, *The Older Hardy* (London: Heinemann, 1978), p. 54. Subsequent references to this work, the second volume of Gittings' fine biography, will be cited *OH.*

15. See Carl J. Weber, *Hardy and the Lady from Madison Square* (Waterville, Me.: Colby College Press, 1952), p. 66.

16. See Oscar Wilde's remark on the use of "morbid" for art criticism: "It is, of course, a ridiculous word to apply to a work of art. For what is morbidity but a mood of emotion or a mode of thought that one cannot express? The public are all morbid, because the public can never find expression for anything. *The artist is never morbid. He expresses everything.* He stands outside his subject and through its medium produces incomparable and artistic effects. To call an artist morbid because he deals with morbidity as a subject-matter is as silly as if one called Shakespeare mad because he wrote *King Lear*." The quotation appears in Wilde's essay "The Soul of Man under Socialism," reprinted in Russel Fraser, ed., *Selected Writings of Oscar Wilde* (Boston: Houghton Mifflin, 1969), p. 352.

17. See Arnold's essay in R. H. Super's splendid edition, *The Complete Prose Works of Matthew Arnold* (Ann Arbor: University of Michigan Press, 1960), 2:19.

18. See Lennart A. Björk, ed., *The Literary Notes of Thomas Hardy* (Göteborg, Sweden: Acta Universitatis Gothoburgensis, 1974), 1:109, for Hardy's transcription of a lengthy portion of Arnold's discussion in his "Heine" essay on the awakening of the modern spirit. Subsequent references to this work are cited *LN*.

19. See Evelyn Hardy and F. B. Pinion, *One Rare Fair Woman* (Coral Gables, Fla.: University of Miami Press, 1972), p. 26.

20. See Hardy's "Apology" to *Late Lyrics and Earlier*, in *CP*, p. 558.

CHAPTER TWO

1. John A. Lester, Jr., *Journey through Despair, 1880–1914* (Princeton, N.J.: Princeton University Press, 1968), p. 4. I am indebted to Lester throughout this paragraph.

2. Forbes Winslow, *The Anatomy of Suicide* (London: Henry Renshaw, 1840), pp. v–vi. Subsequent references to this work will be cited *AS*.

3. These are climate, hereditary predispositions, cerebral injuries, disease of the stomach and liver, complicated with melan-

cholia and hypochondriasis, suppressed secretions, intoxication, unnatural vices, and derangement of the *primae viae* (*AS*, pp. 130–39). In referring to the last condition as a frequent cause of self-destruction, Winslow strikes a light note (in his otherwise solemn study) when he points to the influence of indigestion and bilious disorder upon the spirits and recounts Voltaire's advice to anyone intent on asking a favor of a minister, secretary, or mistress: Be careful to approach them "after they have had a comfortable evacuation from the bowels" (*AS*, pp. 195–96).

4. See *LN*, 1:268–71, for Björk's concise discussion of Hardy's use of this essay. All citations follow Hardy's own form of transcription. While it is impossible to estimate exactly how much an essay influenced an author, it is easy, I think, to *under*estimate the effects of "The Ethics of Suicide" upon Hardy's characterization.

5. Emile Durkheim, *Suicide*, trans. J. A. Spaulding (1897; rpt. Glencoe, Ill.: Free Press, 1951), p. 370. Subsequent references to this work will be cited *S*.

6. Dr. Gregory Zilboorg, in "Suicide among Civilized and Primitive Races" (*American Journal of Psychiatry*, 95 [1935–36]: 18), discussing the public's squeamishness in recognizing suicide and the inadequacy of statistics recording it, reveals the motives that prevent accurate reporting of suicide: desire for religious burial, settlement of insurance claims, and avoidance of such a "stigma" for survivors.

7. See Jacques Choron, *Suicide* (New York: Scribner, 1972), pp. 66–67. Whitney Pope, in *Durkheim's Suicide: A Classic Analyzed* (Chicago: University of Chicago Press, 1976), gives a fine "overview" of the types on pp. 14–29.

8. Quoted in Choron, *Suicide*, p. 68.

9. A good summary of the development of Freud's theories appears in A. Alvarez, *The Savage God: A Study of Suicide* (New York: Bantam Books, 1973), pp. 98–102.

10. Karl A. Menninger, *Man against Himself* (1938; rpt. New York: Harcourt, Brace & World, 1966), p. 73. Subsequent references to this work will be cited *M*.

11. Quoted in *M*, pp. 75 and 37.

12. See *M*, p. 88, and Otto Fenichel, *The Psychoanalytic Theory of Neurosis* (New York: Norton, 1945), p. 401.

13. Christopher Ricks, *Tennyson* (New York: Macmillan, 1972), pp. 102–4 and 108.

14. Quoted in Choron, *Suicide*, p. 31.

15. See especially the two brief treatments of evolutionary meliorism in J. O. Bailey's *Thomas Hardy and the Cosmic Mind* (Chapel Hill: University of North Carolina Press, 1956), pp. 152–81, and "Evolutionary Meliorism in the Poetry of Thomas Hardy," *Studies in Philology*, 60 (July 1963): 569–87.

16. See Hardy's poems "In Tenebris II" (*CP*, #137) and "To Sincerity" (*CP*, #233).

17. All quotations from the novels are from the New Wessex Edition, published by Macmillan London Ltd. in the mid-1970s. Throughout this study I shall use these common abbreviations: *T*, *J*, *FMC*, *MC*, *W*, and *RN* for, respectively, *Tess, Jude, Far from the Madding Crowd, The Mayor of Casterbridge, The Woodlanders*, and *The Return of the Native*. The comment appears in *RN*, p. 205.

CHAPTER THREE

1. See *Thomas Hardy* (Cambridge, Mass.: Harvard University Press, 1949). Guerard's suggestive insights about self-destructiveness are developed in his chapter "Of Men and Women."

2. See Evelyn Hardy, *Thomas Hardy: A Critical Biography* (London, 1954; rpt. New York: Russell & Russell, 1970), pp. 231 and 233.

3. See J. Hillis Miller, *Thomas Hardy: Distance and Desire* (Cambridge, Mass.: Belknap Press, 1970), pp. 196 and 218–19.

4. The opposing positions in the debate are summarized by J. I. M. Stewart in *Thomas Hardy: A Critical Biography* (New York: Dodd, Mead, 1971), pp. 104–5.

5. See Lawrence J. Starzyk, "The Coming Wish Not to Live in Hardy's 'Modern' Novels," *Nineteenth Century Fiction*, 26 (March

1972): 419–35. These figures do not persevere in life: Eustacia commits suicide after two months of marriage, Henchard within months of Elizabeth-Jane's marriage, Jude within months of his children's death and Sue's return to Phillotson. In fact, those who wish *not* to live take direct and effective action to end their lives.

6. See the interesting study by Harry Slochower, "Suicides in Literature: Their Ego Function," *American Imago*, 32 (Winter 1975): 396. Robert Gittings, in *OH* and in personal conversations, has treated the depressing effects of Hardy's intermittent bladder ailment. He considers Hardy's health an important factor for the critical study of some of Hardy's work.

7. See DeLaura, "'The Ache of Modernism,'" p. 396.

8. See the "Heine" essay in Super's edition of Arnold's *Complete Prose Works*, 3:109.

CHAPTER FOUR

1. Robert Evans, "The Other Eustacia," *Novel*, 1 (1968): 251–59, and David Eggenschwiler, "Eustacia Vye, Queen of Night and Courtly Pretender," *Nineteenth Century Fiction*, 25 (1971): 444–54.

2. Bruce K. Martin, "Whatever Happened to Eustacia Vye?" *Studies in the Novel*, 4 (Winter 1972): 619–27.

3. See John Paterson's important monograph on Hardy's revisions, *The Making of The Return of the Native* (Berkeley: University of California Press, 1960).

4. See Gittings, *YH*, pp. 182–83.

5. See Björk, *LN*, 1:48–50.

6. In a footnote to his "'Visible Essences' as Thematic Unity in Hardy's *The Return of the Native*" (*English Studies*, 53 [February 1972]: 7), Björk mentions Eustacia's death in relation to his discussion of Hardy's reading of "The Ethics of Suicide." Admitting the obscurity of the details of her death, Björk says that suicide cannot be ruled out, as the act seems characteristic of her unyielding, defiant nature.

7. See *RN*, p. 41.

8. See Durkheim, *S*, p. 192.

9. See Alvarez, *The Savage God: A Study of Suicide*, p. 104, for his discussion of a suicidal "death trend" in the survivors of parents who have died under dramatic or tragic circumstances.

10. Leonard W. Deen, "Heroism and Pathos in Hardy's *Return of the Native*," *Nineteenth Century Fiction*, 15 (1960): 213.

11. Ibid.

12. See Durkheim's discussion of the "disease of the infinite" (p. 187 in *S*).

13. Deen, "Heroism and Pathos," p. 211.

14. See Menninger, *M*, pp. 144–59. This form of suicide is related to martyrdom.

15. See ibid., p. 63, for a discussion of drowning fantasies as a form of suicide.

16. Alvarez, *The Savage God*, pp. 116–19.

17. Ibid., p. 202.

18. It is not surprising that Eustacia should prefer two powerful leaders and passionate lovers to Wildeve—nor that one is a suicide.

19. Eustacia's last words exemplify the theories of I. Sadger and Paul-Louis Landsberg. Sadger's principle is that "nobody commits suicide who has not given up the hope for love." (See Paul Friedman, ed., *On Suicide* [New York: International Universities Press, 1967], p. 22.) Landsberg argues that "the failure of all means . . . leads to suicide; it is the universal experience of powerlessness. This convergence of one disaster after another, destroying all possibility of living and struggling," is the common factor in suicides. See Landsberg's *The Moral Problem of Suicide*, trans. Cynthia Rowland (London: Rockliff, 1953), p. 95.

20. Ken Zellefrow, "*The Return of the Native:* Hardy's Map and Eustacia's Suicide," *Nineteenth Century Fiction*, 28 (1973): 218. An analogous suicide is described in James Thomson's desperate, nightmarish poem "The City of Dreadful Night" (ll. 966–67): "Another wades in slow with purpose set / Until the waters are above him furled."

21. See Paterson, *Making of The Return of the Native*, p. 165, n. 1.

CHAPTER FIVE

1. See Robert B. Heilman's splendid "Introduction" to *The Mayor of Casterbridge* (Boston: Houghton Mifflin, 1962), pp. v–xl, where he discusses (p. xxxv) Henchard's egoism and the series of acts of separation or banishment that isolate his ego.

2. Guerard, *Thomas Hardy*, pp. 147 and 150. Guerard refers to the work of Karl Menninger and other psychologists and psychoanalysts who have shown that the unfortunate are often the guilty, who must pay daily hostages to their fear.

3. Frederick R. Karl considers Henchard's "seeming impetuousness in ignoring all advice as more than mere rashness or ill temper. It is the chief constituent of an innate need to debase himself, to act out a role that will ultimately diminish him." See his fine essay, "*The Mayor of Casterbridge*: A New Fiction Defined," *Modern Fiction Studies*, 6 (Autumn 1960): 195–213.

4. See Menninger, *M*, pp. 50–57.

5. Guerard, *Thomas Hardy*, pp. 147–48, says that the guilty not only "flagellate themselves but also thrust themselves in the way of bad luck: *create* what appear to be unlucky accidents."

6. See ibid., p. 151. Also see Menninger on "focal" suicide (*M*, pp. 229ff.).

7. See Julian Moynahan's suggestive essay, "*The Mayor of Casterbridge* and the Old Testament's First Book of Samuel: A Study of Some Literary Relationships," *Publications of the Modern Language Association*, 71 (1956): 118–30.

8. Henchard's failure to dispatch his enemy might be explained by the fact that melancholiacs "rarely kill anyone but themselves, although their driving motive is the wish to kill someone else" (Menninger, *M*, p. 55).

9. "The tendency to put an end to one's life not instantaneously by one heroic act, but by a series of deprivations" is called "chronic suicide" by Dr. Stekel. See Friedman, ed., *On Suicide*, p. 90.

10. See Jean Brooks, *Thomas Hardy: The Poetic Structure* (Ithaca, N.Y.: Cornell University Press, 1971), p. 199: "Henchard's impulse to self-punishment places him in the way of bad luck."

11. See Durkheim, *S*, pp. 271 and 285.

12. For Stekel's discussion, see Friedman, ed., *On Suicide*, pp. 90–91.

13. Discussed by Menninger in *M*, pp. 78–79.

14. See his poems "Her Immortality" and "His Immortality," in *CP*, numbers 32 and 109 respectively.

CHAPTER SIX

1. The unicorn, a traditional symbol of chastity and fierceness, virginity and the power of love, becomes a gentle mate after being tamed by the touch of a virgin. See Maria Leach, ed., *Standard Dictionary of Folklore Mythology and Legend* (New York: Funk and Wagnalls, 1972), p. 1150. Clearly, Hardy is teasing us into attention when he has Bathsheba reject the seal with a unicorn's head because "there's nothing in that." There's far more in it about Boldwood than she can see at that time.

2. Durkheim defines anomie as the condition of deregulation caused by disturbances and disorganization in the social organism to which the individual belongs (i.e., the family, religious group, body politic, profession, etc.). Such disturbances, in which the individual's horizon is broadened beyond what he can endure, or is contracted unduly, release social forces for which the individual lacks experience. His need for reduction in his requirements, restraining his needs, learning self-control, takes time, so that, for some individuals, the "new life" becomes intolerable and their separation from an integrated existence leads to anomic suicide.

See Durkheim's "anatomy" of the anomic suicide (pp. 241–76 in *S*).

3. In *The Savage God*, Alvarez treats the "closed world" of the suicide and his childishness (pp. 75–132 and 202).

4. Sigmund Freud, in "Mourning and Melancholia" (*Collected Papers* [New York: Basic Books, 1959] 4:157), says the chief loss suffered by the melancholiac is his self-respect; he is victimized by his conscience and experiences moral dissatisfaction with the self.

5. See ibid., p. 153.

6. See Durkheim, *S*, pp. 284–85.

7. Paul-Louis Landsberg's discussion of suicide as the keystone of the Stoic philosophy (in *The Moral Problem of Suicide*, pp. 71–92) seems relevant to my treatment of Boldwood's choice of self-destruction.

8. Earl A. Grollman (in *Suicide* [Boston: Beacon Press, 1971], p. 72) writes: "Suicide does not occur suddenly, or impulsively, or unpredictably, or inevitably. It is the final step of a progressive failure of adaptation."

9. Freud, "Mourning and Melancholia", 4:153–63. Menninger discusses the three components in the suicidal act: the wish to kill (aggression), the wish to be killed (submission), and the wish to die. The first component is obviously met in Boldwood's attack on Troy and, secondly, we have previously heard Boldwood express the desire to die (p. 270); moreover, his last words reiterate components (or motives) 1 and 2. Finally, his submission to the law, after his failed attempt at suicide, can be seen as an alternative mode of seeking his own death.

CHAPTER SEVEN

1. These comments appear in the "Preface" to the first edition and in the 1912 "Postscript."

2. See *Notes from Underground*, reprinted in Walter Kaufmann, *Existentialism from Dostoevsky to Sartre* (Cleveland and New York: World, 1956), p. 56.

3. See my essay "*Jude the Obscure* and the *Bildungsroman*," *Studies in the Novel*, 4 (Winter 1972): 580–91.

4. See Ian Gregor, "*Jude the Obscure*," in Maynard Mack and Ian Gregor, eds., *Imagined Worlds: Essays on Some English Novels and Novelists in Honour of John Butt* (London: Methuen, 1968), p. 238.

5. From Heine's "Götterdämmerung," quoted in *J*, p. 137.

6. From Robert Browning's "The Statue and the Bust," quoted in *J*, p. 253.

7. See Jude's allusion to Romans 8:38–39. When he says that nothing can divide him from Sue, he recalls Paul's claim that nothing can "separate us from the love of God."

8. See Durkheim (*S*, pp. 189–202) on the effects of marriage for reducing one's vulnerability to suicide.

9. See Ward Hellstrom, "*Jude the Obscure* as Pagan Self-Assertion," *Victorian Newsletter*, no. 29 (Spring 1966), p. 27.

10. See Sue's later judgment of him: "Remember that the best and greatest among mankind are those who do themselves no worldly good. Every successful man is more or less a selfish man. The devoted fail. . . . 'Charity seeketh not her own'" (p. 369).

11. See Alvarez's "Afterword" to the Signet edition of *Jude* (New York: New American Library, 1961), p. 411.

12. See "*Jude the Obscure:* Hardy's Symbolic Indictment of Christianity," *Nineteenth Century Fiction*, 9 (June 1954): 50–60.

13. See Hellstrom, "*Jude the Obscure* as Pagan Self-Assertion," p. 27.

14. See John Stuart Mill, *On Liberty*, reprinted in *Essential Works of John Stuart Mill*, ed. Max Lerner (New York: Bantam Books, 1961), p. 311.

15. See Kierkegaard's *Either/Or*, trans. Walter Lowrie (Garden City, N.Y.: Doubleday, 1959), 2:217. I am indebted to Ward Hellstrom, to his essay and conversations, for suggesting this line of inquiry.

16. Søren Kierkegaard, *The Sickness unto Death*, in *Fear and Trembling and The Sickness unto Death*, trans. Walter Lowrie (Garden City, N.Y.: Doubleday, 1954), p. 201.

17. See *Meditations,* in *Marcus Aurelius Meditations—Epictetus Enchiridion,* introd. Russell Kirk (South Bend, Ind.: Gateway, 1956), p. 29.

18. See Epicurus, *Morals,* trans. Walter Charleton (London: P. Davis, 1926), p. 77.

19. See Charleton's "An Apology for Epicurus" in his trans. of Epicurus' *Morals* (n.p.).

20. See Epicurus, *Morals,* in Charleton trans., p. 79.

21. See Berdyaev, *Slavery and Freedom,* in *Four Existentialist Theologians,* ed. Will Herberg (Garden City, N.Y.: Doubleday, 1958), p. 116.

22. See Barzun, "Truth and Poetry in Thomas Hardy," *Southern Review,* 4 (Fall 1940): 188.

CHAPTER EIGHT

1. See the letter to Leslie Stephen, quoted in *L,* p. 100.

2. The claim, made in the novel's first chapter, is rightly called into question by Ian Gregor in *The Great Web: The Form of Hardy's Major Fiction* (Totowa, N.J.: Rowman and Littlefield, 1974), p. 139.

3. See Kramer, *Thomas Hardy: The Forms of Tragedy,* p. 93.

4. Hardy renders her ambivalence when he describes Grace as a civilized young lady who craves to be a country girl again—an impressionable creature who combines "modern" nerves with primitive feelings (see pp. 300 and 309). Her divided consciousness—the conflict within her between nature and civilization, simplicity and sophistication—prevents her from making effective decisions until after Giles is dead.

5. There is the analogous situation in *Hard Times,* where Jem determines, as a means of eluding his langor and boredom, to make Louisa love him. The pursuit has all the interest of a hunt, where the victim is presumed to have no emotions or personal importance.

6. See Durkheim, *S*, pp. 220–25 and 283.

7. See the early description of Gabriel Oak: no longer a young man at twenty-eight, and a bachelor, but a man whose "intellect and . . . emotions were clearly separated" (*FFMC*, pp. 42–43).

8. See *L*, p. 170, where Lady Camilla Portsmith is identified as the woman who provided this insight for Hardy.

9. See Roy Morrell's fine study of Gabriel Oak in his *Thomas Hardy: The Will and the Way* (Kuala Lumpur: University of Malaya Press, 1965).

10. See Freud's classical analysis in "Mourning and Melancholia" (pp. 153–63).

11. See ibid., pp. 155–58.

12. See ibid., p. 158, and Freud's treatment of the melancholiac's displacement of his anger against his loved one.

13. See Irving Howe, *Thomas Hardy* (New York: Macmillan, 1967), p. 104.

14. See Menninger's treatment of asceticism and martyrdom (*M*, pp. 88–142).

15. See ibid., pp. 125 and 344.

16. See Durkheim, *S*, p. 283.

CHAPTER NINE

1. Furbank's "Introduction" to the New Wessex Edition of *Tess of the d'Urbervilles* (London and Basingstroke: Macmillan, 1974), p. 20. Also see Howe's *Thomas Hardy*, pp. 110–12.

2. Hardy writes here of "The 'appetite for joy' which pervades all creation, that tremendous force which sways humanity to its purpose, as the tide sways the helpless reed," which induces Tess to accept Angel. But the full context of this acceptance includes Tess's wish that she had never been born, the description of the lovers as driving "through the gloom," and her fear that his refusal to dance with her at the Marlott club-walking is no ill omen for them now. As matters develop, Tess's fear *is* realized.

3. See especially Evelyn Hardy, *Thomas Hardy: A Critical Biography*, pp. 231–35. While Miss Hardy's perceptive remarks provide a truer, more balanced view of Tess, many "lovers" of Tess—that is, readers who feel as warmly toward her as to a living person—prefer to ignore or deemphasize the self-destructive element in Tess's nature. That she inspires such a generous feeling is rare testimony to her goodness and vitality, but that feeling leads to an incomplete response to her complex character, I believe.

4. In this perception and in the working out of Tess's fate, Hardy exactly represents Freud's central intention in *Civilization and Its Discontents:* "to show that the price we pay for our advance in civilization is a loss of happiness through the heightening of the sense of guilt" (p. 81 in James Strachey's edition [New York: Norton, 1962]).

5. In *Thomas Hardy: Distance and Desire* (Cambridge, Mass.: Belknap Press, 1970) J. Hillis Miller gives fine treatment to Hardy's characters' solution to the problem of living without God in the world. They require a lover to take the place of an "absent" or "dead" God, so that the ensuing, intense pressure upon the relationship, created by a lover's being forced to be what he or she is not, leads to failure of the union and the suffering of the lovers.

6. See Menninger (*M*, pp. 83 and 91) for his distinctions between the two extreme types of martyrs.

7. See Evelyn Hardy, *Thomas Hardy: A Critical Biography*, p. 233.

8. See pp. 267, 274, 276, and 278 in the text.

9. See pp. 241 and 268 in the text.

10. But see her first letter, where she claims that the punishment he has measured out to her is well deserved. My point is not that Tess is illogical, but that she is deeply divided in her impulses and perceptions. Angel's punishment of her seems just or unjust, insofar as her impulse to live or die is uppermost.

11. See Evelyn Hardy, *Thomas Hardy: A Critical Biography*, p. 234.

12. See Durkheim, *S*, p. 283.

CHAPTER TEN

1. See Harold Orel, *The Final Years of Thomas Hardy, 1912–1928* (Lawrence: University Press of Kansas, 1976), p. 126.

2. See David Daiches, *Some Late Victorian Attitudes* (London: André Deutsch, 1969), p. 9.

3. See Morse Peckham, *Victorian Revolutionaries: Speculations on Some Heroes of a Culture Crisis* (New York: George Braziller, 1970), p. 71.

4. See DeLaura, "'The Ache of Modernism,'" p. 399.

5. See Hardy's "Apology" to *Late Lyrics and Earlier* (*CP*, p. 561).

Bibliography

ALVAREZ, A. "Afterword" to *Jude the Obscure*. New York: New American Library, 1961.

―――. *The Savage God: A Study of Suicide*. New York: Bantam Books, 1973.

ARNOLD, MATTHEW. *The Complete Prose Works of Matthew Arnold*. Ed. R. H. Super. 11 vols. Ann Arbor: University of Michigan Press, 1960―77.

AURELIUS, MARCUS. *Meditations*. In *Marcus Aurelius Meditations―Epictetus Enchiridion*. Introd. Russell Kirk. South Bend, Ind.: Gateway Editions, 1956.

BAILEY, J. O. "Evolutionary Meliorism in the Poetry of Thomas Hardy," *Studies in Philology*, 60 (July 1963): 569―87.

―――. *Thomas Hardy and the Cosmic Mind*. Chapel Hill: University of North Carolina Press, 1956.

BARZUN, JACQUES. "Truth and Poetry in Thomas Hardy," *Southern Review*, 4 (Fall 1940): 179―92.

BERDYAEV, NICHOLAS. *Slavery and Freedom*. In *Four Existentialist Theologians*, ed. Will Herberg. Garden City, N.Y.: Doubleday, 1958.

BJÖRK, LENNART A., ed. *The Literary Notes of Thomas Hardy*. Göteborg, Sweden: Acta Universitatis Gothoburgensis, 1974.

————. "'Visible Essences' as Thematic Unity in Hardy's *The Re-turn of the Native*," *English Studies*, 53 (February 1972): 1–12.

BROOKS, JEAN. *Thomas Hardy: The Poetic Structure*. Ithaca, N.Y.: Cornell University Press, 1971.

CHORON, JACQUES. *Suicide*. New York: Charles Scribner's Sons, 1972.

DAICHES, DAVID. *Some Late Victorian Attitudes*. London: André Deutsch, 1969.

DEEN, LEONARD W. "Heroism and Pathos in Hardy's *The Return of the Native*," *Nineteenth Century Fiction*, 15 (1960): 207–19.

DELAURA, DAVID J. "'The Ache of Modernism' in Hardy's Later Novels," *Journal of English Literary History*, 34 (1967): 380–99.

DOSTOEVSKY, FEODOR. *Notes from Underground*. Trans. Constance Garnett. In *Existentialism from Dostoevsky to Sartre*, ed. Walter Kaufmann. Cleveland and New York: World Publishing Co., 1956.

DURKHEIM, EMILE. *Suicide*. Trans. J. A. Spaulding and George Simpson. Glencoe, Ill.: Free Press, 1951 (original pub. 1897).

EGGENSCHWILER, DAVID. "Eustacia Vye, Queen of Night and Courtly Pretender," *Nineteenth Century Fiction*, 25 (1971): 444–54.

EVANS, ROBERT. "The Other Eustacia," *Novel*, 1 (1968): 251–59.

FENICHEL, OTTO. *The Psychoanalytic Theory of Neurosis*. New York: W. W. Norton, 1945.

FREUD, SIGMUND. "Mourning and Melancholia," *Collected Papers*. Vol. 4. New York: Basic Books, 1959.

————. *Civilization and Its Discontents*. Ed. James Strachey. New York: W. W. Norton, 1962.

FRIEDMAN, PAUL, ed. *On Suicide*. New York: International Universities Press, 1967.

FURBANK, P. N. "Introduction" to *Tess of the D'Urbervilles*. London and Basingstoke: Macmillan London, 1974.

GIBSON, JAMES, ed. *The Complete Poems of Thomas Hardy*. London: Macmillan London, 1976.
GITTINGS, ROBERT. *The Older Hardy*. London: Heinemann, 1978.
————. *Young Thomas Hardy*. London: Heinemann, 1975.
GREGOR, IAN. *The Great Web: The Form of Hardy's Major Fiction*. Totowa, N.J.: Rowman and Littlefield, 1974.
————. "Jude the Obscure," in Maynard Mack and Ian Gregor, eds., *Imagined Worlds: Essays on Some English Novels and Novelists in Honour of John Butt*. London: Methuen, 1968.
GROLLMAN, EARL A. *Suicide*. Boston: Beacon Press, 1971.
GUERARD, ALBERT J. *Thomas Hardy*. Cambridge, Mass.: Harvard University Press, 1949.
HARDY, EVELYN. *Thomas Hardy: A Critical Biography*. New York: Russell & Russell, 1970 (original pub. 1954).
———— and F. B. Pinion. *One Rare Fair Woman: Thomas Hardy's Letters to Florence Henniker, 1893–1922*. Coral Gables, Fla.: University of Miami Press, 1972.
HARDY, FLORENCE EMILY. *The Life of Thomas Hardy*. London: Macmillan, 1962.
HARDY, THOMAS. *Complete Poems of Thomas Hardy*. Ed. James Gibson. London: Macmillan London, 1976.
————. *Far from the Madding Crowd*. Introd. John Bayley. London: Macmillan London, 1975.
————. *Jude the Obscure*. Introd. Terry Eagleton. London: Macmillan London, 1974.
————. *The Mayor of Casterbridge*. Introd. Ian Gregor. London: Macmillan London, 1975.
————. *Personal Writings of Thomas Hardy*. Ed. Harold Orel. Lawrence: University of Kansas Press, 1966.
————. *The Return of the Native*. Introd. Derwent May. London: Macmillan London, 1975.
————. *Tess of the D'Urbervilles*. Introd. P. N. Furbank. London: Macmillan London, 1974.
————. *The Woodlanders*. Introd. David Lodge. London: Macmillan London, 1974.

HEILMAN, ROBERT B. "Introduction" to *The Mayor of Casterbridge*. Boston: Houghton Mifflin, 1962.

HELLSTROM, WARD. *"Jude the Obscure* as Pagan Self-Assertion," *Victorian Newsletter*, no. 29 (Spring 1966), pp. 26–27.

HOLLAND, NORMAN. *"Jude the Obscure*: Hardy's Symbolic Indictment of Christianity," *Nineteenth Century Fiction*, 9 (June 1954): 50–60.

HOWE, IRVING. *Thomas Hardy*. New York: Macmillan, 1967.

KARL, FREDERICK R. *"The Mayor of Casterbridge*: A New Fiction Defined," *Modern Fiction Studies*, 6 (Autumn 1960): 195–213.

KIERKEGAARD, SØREN. *Either/Or*. Trans. Walter Lowrie. Garden City, N.Y.: Doubleday, 1959.

————. *Sickness unto Death*. In *Fear and Trembling and Sickness unto Death*. Trans. Walter Lowrie. Garden City, N.Y.: Doubleday, 1954.

KRAMER, DALE. *Thomas Hardy: The Forms of Tragedy*. Detroit: Wayne State University Press, 1975.

LANDSBERG, PAUL-LOUIS. *The Moral Problem of Suicide*. Trans. Cynthia Rowland. London: Rockliff, 1953.

LEACH, MARIA, ed. *Standard Dictionary of Folklore, Mythology and Legend*. New York: Funk and Wagnalls, 1972.

LESTER, JOHN A. *Journey through Despair, 1880–1914*. Princeton, N.J.: Princeton University Press, 1968.

MARTIN, BRUCE K. "Whatever Happened to Eustacia Vye?" *Studies in the Novel*, 4 (Winter 1972): 619–27.

MENNINGER, KARL A. *Man against Himself*. New York: Harcourt, Brace & World, 1966 (original pub. 1938).

MILL, JOHN STUART. *On Liberty*. In *Essential Works of John Stuart Mill*. Ed. Max Lerner. New York: Bantam Books, 1961.

MILLER, J. HILLIS. *Thomas Hardy: Distance and Desire*. Cambridge, Mass.: Belknap Press, 1970.

MILLGATE, MICHAEL. *Thomas Hardy: A Biography*. New York: Random House, 1982.

———. *Thomas Hardy: His Career as a Novelist*. New York: Random House, 1971.

——— and Richard Little Purdy, eds. *The Collected Letters of Thomas Hardy*. Oxford: Clarendon Press, 1978–82.

MORRELL, ROY. *Thomas Hardy: The Will and the Way*. Kuala Lumpur: University of Malaya Press, 1965.

MOYNAHAN, JULIAN. "*The Mayor of Casterbridge* and the Old Testament's First Book of Samuel: A Study of Some Literary Relationships," *Publications of the Modern Language Association*, 71 (March 1956): 118–30.

OREL, HAROLD. *The Final Years of Thomas Hardy, 1912–1928*. Lawrence: University Press of Kansas, 1976.

———, ed. *Thomas Hardy's Personal Writings*. Lawrence: University of Kansas Press, 1966.

PATERSON, JOHN. *The Making of The Return of the Native*. Berkeley: University of California Press, 1960.

PECKHAM, MORSE. *Victorian Revolutionaries: Speculations on Some Heroes of a Culture Crisis*. New York: George Braziller, 1970.

POPE, WHITNEY. *Durkheim's Suicide: A Classic Analyzed*. Chicago: University of Chicago Press, 1976.

RICKS, CHRISTOPHER. *Tennyson*. New York: Macmillan, 1972.

SLOCHOWER, HARRY. "Suicides in Literature: Their Ego Function," *American Imago*, 32 (Winter 1975): 389–416.

STARZYK, LAWRENCE J. "The Coming Wish Not to Live in Hardy's 'Modern' Novels," *Nineteenth Century Fiction*, 26 (March 1972): 419–35.

STEWART, J. I. M. *Thomas Hardy: A Critical Biography*. New York: Dodd, Mead, 1971.

WEBER, CARL J. *Hardy and the Lady from Madison Square*. Waterville, Me.: Colby College Press, 1952.

WILDE, OSCAR. "The Soul of Man under Socialism," in *Selected Writings of Oscar Wilde*. Ed. Russell Fraser. Boston: Houghton Mifflin, 1969.

WINSLOW, FORBES. *The Anatomy of Suicide*. London: Henry Renshaw, 1840.

ZELLEFROW, KEN. *"The Return of the Native*: Hardy's Map and Eustacia's Suicide," *Nineteenth Century Fiction*, 28 (1973): 214–20.

ZILBOORG, GREGORY. "Suicide among Civilized and Primitive Races," *American Journal of Psychiatry*, vol. 95 (1935–36).

Index